GOLF

About the Authors

Virginia Nance is a Class A and Life Member of the Ladies Professional Golf Association (LPGA). She has given both class and private lessons to boys and girls, men and women, in high schools, at practice golf ranges, in camps, and at colleges and universities, and has participated in or conducted golf clinics at local, state, and national levels. She has competed in various amateur tournaments, including the U.S. Amateur for Women.

Formerly a teacher at the University of Southern California, Nance has contributed articles to publications of the National Association for Girls and Women in Sports (NAGWS) and the American Alliance for Health, Physical Education, Recreation, and Dance (AAHPERD). She holds degrees from the University of Illinois and the University of Wisconsin, Madison and has completed further graduate work at the University of Southern California.

The late Dr. Elwood Craig Davis was a well-known and distinguished professor of physical education, having been associated with such major institutions as Pennsylvania State University, University of Pittsburgh, University of Louisville, and professor emeritus at University of Southern California. His last teaching was at California State University at Northridge. His honors are legion, the most outstanding perhaps being a recipient of the Phi Epsilon Kappa National Award and both the American Academy of Physical Education's Hetherington Award and the AAHPERD's Luther Halsey Gulick Medal.

Dr. Davis graduated from the University of Washington, University of Chicago, and Columbia University. Service was in U.S. Naval Aviation and Naval Physical Training. He also authored or coauthored nine books and numerous articles.

Kay McMahon is a Class A member of both the LPGA and the Professional Golfers' Association of America. A teaching professional at a golf club, she has been honored twice by the Western Section of the LPGA with the "Teacher of the Year" award. She has conducted and participated in many teaching workshops and clinics. Her career in competitive golf has included play in amateur and professional tournaments.

McMahon holds a degree in physical education from the University of Minnesota, Duluth. Besides her busy teaching schedule, she contributes to the work of the LPGA, writes golf articles, and is active in community affairs.

GOLF
Seventh Edition

Virginia Lindblad Nance
Life Member, Ladies Professional Golf Association,
Western Section; Formerly of University of Southern California

Elwood Craig Davis (deceased)
Professor Emeritus, Formerly of University of Southern California

Kay E. McMahon
Member, Ladies Professional Golf Association
and Professional Golfers' Association of America

Illustrations by Lorrie Powell, Denise Powell, and Ruth Schonhorst

WCB Brown & Benchmark
P U B L I S H E R S

Madison, Wisconsin • Dubuque, Iowa • Indianapolis, Indiana
Melbourne, Australia • Oxford, England

Book Team

Executive Editor *Ed Bartell*
Editor *Scott Spoolman*
Production Editor *Peggy Selle*
Visuals/Design Developmental Consultant *Marilyn A. Phelps*
Visuals/Design Freelance Specialist *Mary L. Christianson*
Publishing Services Specialist *Sherry Padden*
Marketing Manager *Pamela S. Cooper*
Advertising Manager *Jodi Rymer*

WCB Brown & Benchmark

A Division of Wm. C. Brown Communications, Inc.

Executive Vice President/General Manager *Thomas E. Doran*
Vice President/Editor in Chief *Edgar J. Laube*
Vice President/Sales and Marketing *Eric Ziegler*
Director of Production *Vickie Putman Caughron*
Director of Custom and Electronic Publishing *Chris Rogers*

WCB Wm. C. Brown Communications, Inc.

President and Chief Executive Officer *G. Franklin Lewis*
Corporate Senior Vice President and Chief Financial Officer *Robert Chesterman*
Corporate Senior Vice President and President of Manufacturing *Roger Meyer*

Consulting Editor
Physical Educatiuon
Aileene Lockhart
Texas Woman's University

Sports and Fitness Series Evaluation Materials Editor
Jane A. Mott
Texas Woman's University

Cover design by Regan Design

Cover image by Jon Feingersh/The Stock Market

Copyedited by Mary Monner

A Times Mirror Company

Library of Congress Catalog Card Number: 92–75967

ISBN 0–697–12656–0

Printed in the United States of America by Wm. C. Brown Communications, Inc.,
2460 Kerper Boulevard, Dubuque, IA 52001

10 9 8 7 6 5 4 3 2 1

Contents

Preface

This seventh edition of *Golf* is a guide to help players become better golfers: to develop and to improve skill in the golf strokes, thereby assuring lower golf scores; and to become complete golfers, knowledgeable in the many aspects of the total game.

The general outline for presenting the strokes has been retained. The writing and illustrations have been carefully examined, with additions and changes for clarity.

This book is not *just* for beginners. Only the first chapter deals with the elementary aspects of the game. Information presented in succeeding chapters on fundamentals of the swing and other phases of golf applies to all golfers, no matter their level of experience or expertise.

The text continues to emphasize the basic idea of swinging the club with the purpose of stroking the ball to a target. In seeking "magic" answers to improving their strokes, too many players focus on details of the swing and abandon the fundamentals. In so doing, they become confused and frustrated. Peak performances occur when little or no thought is given to details—when players do not have to think about what they are doing but rather think only of striking the ball to a target.

This book urges players to follow the practices of experts: to ingrain a swing that is based on fundamentals, to work on tempo and rhythm, and to develop a consistent swing. Information presented on the swing concepts, cues for swinging the club, corrections for common errors, and many practice suggestions can help players to improve their games. Readers also will find many positive and useful ideas for playing golf—strategy on the course, along with the important mental side of the game.

The rules summary presented in the book is up-to-date. However, all golfers should own and study the *United States Golf Association Rule Book* for a complete and thorough knowledge of the rules. The rules test at the end of the book will be a challenge to all golfers.

Points of golf etiquette in this book may be the most extensive in print. Following them will make you a class golfer—welcomed and appreciated by all players. Golfing experiences, which should be pleasant, can become unpleasant if accidents occur. Thus, the safety precautions discussed here, and which seldom are presented in writing, are important to all golfers.

To learn about the history of golf, reference books are useful, but nothing can surpass the enjoyment of reading the works of writers and golfers who lived in and described golf's historic years. Thus, this book, unable to do justice to the history of golf in a few paragraphs, contains no historical data.

Because so many theories about the golf game exist, no single book is all-inclusive. Readers should not conclude that concepts and ideas omitted from this book are necessarily questioned or rejected by the authors.

A survey of instructors teaching golf in colleges and universities found that, of the 80 percent who use a textbook, 51 percent use this book. More than a half-million students of the game of golf have now read and studied this book.

Acknowledgments

We would like to thank the golf professionals and the sporting goods companies who granted us permission to include useful pictures in this book. For swing sequence pictures: Sam Snead and Keith Fergus, Wilson Sporting Goods Company; Pat Bradley, Member of Team Mazda, Representative Yamaha Golf Company; Beth Stone, former LPGA Tour player; Ayako Okamoto and Ricky Kawagishi, Mizuno Golf Company; Jim Booros, Acushnet Golf Equipment; Ed Fiori, PGA Tour member for thirteen years. For pictures of golf clubs: Tom Crowe, Cobra Golf Company; George Nichols, Square Two Golf Company.

Further thanks go to Cecile Hemphill for the use of pictures of Michael Hemphill. Also, we appreciate the permission to include pictures of Doreen La Donna.

The critical reviews of all or part of the text by teachers and golfers are greatly appreciated. Careful note was taken of all their comments, and many of their suggestions and criticisms have been incorporated.

Elwood Craig Davis coauthored the first edition and contributed to some of the succeeding ones. The present senior author, Virginia Nance, would like to acknowledge and also express deep appreciation for the important work of a good friend. His "red-penciling" of manuscripts will not be forgotten.

The Game of Golf

1

You are either one of the millions of people playing golf or you soon will be. It is not necessary to "sell" golf. The advantages of knowing how to play are evident. Ever-increasing numbers of people choose to learn the game, and once learned, golf becomes an enjoyable lifetime recreation.

Golf requires no special physical attributes. An average amount of flexibility, agility, endurance, and coordination may well produce a better-than-average golfer—or an excellent player. People learn this sport at any age. True, golf is not a simple game, but becoming proficient in any motor skill takes dedication.

In golf, fears of failing to perform well are unjustified. All players sample the joy of hitting fine golf shots. These moments of pleasure increase with practice and play. A wave of poor shots may crop up in any golfer's play, but these errant strokes are challenges that only heighten a player's spirit and desire. With correct concepts and intelligent practice, you can develop a good golf game.

A Challenge Requiring Self-Discipline and Concentration

Golf is a personal game. From the time the ball is hit from the first teeing ground until it is removed from the hole on the eighteenth green, players are in command of their own games. There is no reaction to someone else's play, such as in tennis and handball. In golf, if the ball is missed completely or is poorly hit, the incident cannot be dismissed, as in some sports, by saying that the opponent hit a superb shot. No excuses are allowed. But when golfers hit excellent shots, they are rewarded—they can claim credit for fine play.

Golf is played in a quiet atmosphere where players may be sensitive to everything both inside and outside themselves. Having time to think in silent surroundings adds a singular dimension—one demanding concentration and self-discipline. A shot is seldom played without some thought. This is not the case in many games, where brilliant plays may be or must be executed as a result of rapid-fire reaction only. Golfers must plan their play, control their thinking, and initiate and complete the action to play each shot. They have time to be introspective, which can be either a detriment or an advantage. They can even "talk" themselves into a bad shot, or a good shot.

Directing the thinking process is a necessity and a real exercise in self-control. Anxious or negative thoughts, fearful of the shot result, must be avoided or blocked out; positive thoughts with trust for a good shot must be embraced. Before the stroke is taken, the thinking mind plans the shot and instills confidence; then this mind must be quieted and relinquish its control to the subconscious for automatic performance. The execution of the shot should proceed at once, with no thought interjected and no plan changed. This is not a simple task.

The physical and mental aspects of golf are interwoven. Together they make a golf game. Hitting good shots is always a challenge and, when accomplished, is always a joy.

The Game

The object of golf is to play a round, usually 18 holes, in as few strokes as possible. At the beginning of each hole (the *tee* or *teeing ground*), the ball may be placed on a peg (*tee*) so it is slightly elevated from the turf. After the ball is struck from the tee, *it is a cardinal rule of golf that the ball be played as it lies on the ground* (except as otherwise provided by the rules). Generally, four golfers, commonly called a *foursome,* play in a group. These players, after teeing off, continue playing their shots in turn (farthest from the hole playing first) until they stroke each of their golf balls into the hole (*cup*). The hole is sunk in a carpet-like area, the *putting green. A flagstick* is placed in the center of the cup so that the position of the hole can be seen from a distance. Some courses have the hole number printed on the pennant of the stick.

The area of closely mowed grass between the tee and the putting green is called the *fairway.* The game would be relatively simple if the ball had to be played only from the tee, the fairway, and the putting green. But such is not the case. If a shot is hit off line and off the fairway, the ball is likely to be found among trees and in long, thick grass—the *rough.* Also, such *hazards* as *lakes, creeks,* and *bunkers* (sand traps) lie ready to engulf misjudged and errant shots. (See fig. 1.1.)

After play on each hole is completed, the number of strokes a player has taken is recorded on the score card. Scores are added for the first and second nine holes (*front* and *back 9's*) and then totaled for the 18-hole score.

Par—The Ever-Present Opponent

Par scores are good scores. The score card shows the par for each hole, the total for both nines, and the 18-hole total. Experienced golfers aim to shoot par or less on each hole.

Interesting terms are used to describe scores in relation to par for a hole. Check the score card (fig. 1.2) for these scores: on hole 13, a score of 3 (1 under par) is a *birdie;* on hole 17, a score of 2 (2 under par) is an *eagle;* on hole 7, a score of 4 (1 over par) is a *bogey. A double bogey* is 2 over par. An exceptionally good score, rarer than a hole-in-one, is a *double eagle* (3 under par).

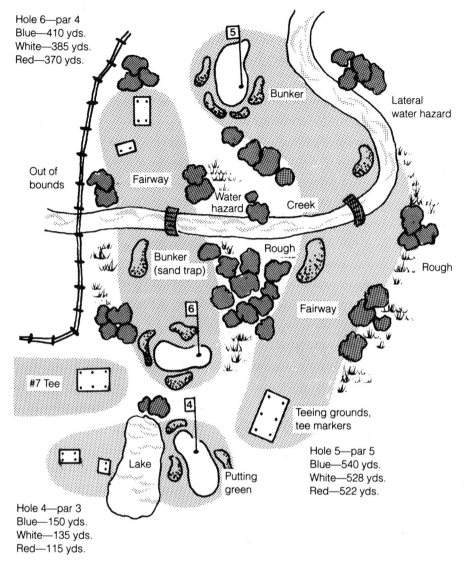

Figure 1.1
Three golf holes.

The major guide in determining par for a hole is its length. The number of strokes a good player needs to hit the ball onto the putting green is figured and then two strokes are added for play on the green. On the average, men hit the ball farther than women do, so women's par will differ from men's par on some of the holes (see table 1.1). The difficulty of the hole is also considered in setting par.

	1	2	3	4	5	6	7	8	9	Out	10	11	12	13	14	15	16	17	18	In	Total		
Blue Course	428	376	390	150	540	410	187	510	375	3366	520	340	200	430	495	180	450	375	395	3385	6751	**Course Rating‡**	
White Course	415	354	370	135	528	385	177	500	355	3219	505	335	190	420	490	175	430	370	380	3295	6514	Blue 71.2	
Par (Men)	4	4	4	3	5	4	3	5	4	36	5	4	3	4	5	3	4	4	4	36	72	White (men) 69.1 White (women) 74.1	
Handicap*	5	15	9	17	1	7	13	3	11		2	18	10	6	4	14	8	16	12			Red 72.2	
Hole Number	1	2	3	4	5	6	7	8	9	Out	10	11	12	13	14	15	16	17	18	In	Total	Hdcp.†	Net
Red Course	398	342	356	115	522	370	149	455	340	3047	495	330	180	398	480	120	385	350	375	3123	6150	**Slope Rating‡** Blue 136	
Par (Women)	4	4	4	3	5	4	3	5	4	36	5	4	3	4	5	3	4	4	4	36	72	White (men) 130 White (women) 134	
Handicap*	3	11	7	17	1	9	13	5	15		4	16	8	6	2	18	12	10	14			Red 126	

* Handicap—These numbers represent the playing difficulty of a hole. Hole 5 is considered most difficult on all three courses—Blue, White, and Red. Hole 11 on the Blue and White courses and Hole 15 on the Red course are rated the least difficult holes.

†Hdcp.—A player's handicap; to be subtracted from the gross score to compute the net score.

‡Course and Slope Ratings—Evaluations of the playing difficulty of a course.

Figure 1.2
Score card.

Table 1.1   Yardage guidelines for par computation.

Women		Men	
Par		Par	
3	Up to 210 yards	3	Up to 250 yards
4	211–400 yards	4	251–470 yards
5	401–575 yards	5	471 yards and over
6	576 yards and over		

Golf Courses

Much expert knowledge and work go into planning, building, and maintaining a golf course. Sometimes, the playing of the game is so absorbing or exasperating that the beauty and design of a golf course are momentarily forgotten. Golf requires the largest playing field of any modern game. All courses and all holes differ. Golf course architects design courses to challenge players to hit their best shots and to penalize them if they fail to do so. The designers lay out the courses, taking full advantage of the topography, the beauty of nature, and the outdoors.

On what may be called standard for a golf course, holes vary in length from about 100 yards to about 600 yards. Since golf does not have an exact regulation playing field, golfers must continually adapt their games to the peculiarities of each course, which may, in itself, vary in length and challenge from day to day.

To protect the turf on the teeing grounds and around the holes on the putting greens, the positions of the tee markers and the holes are changed often. If the teeing grounds and putting greens are large, the placement of both the tee markers and the holes can make a significant difference in the difficulty and length of each hole.

Most golf courses have more than one teeing ground per hole—in some cases, three or more. Those having three sets of teeing grounds may designate the areas with different-colored markers, such as blue for the back tee, white for the middle tee, and red for the forward tee. Expert men golfers are likely to shoot from the blue tees, average players from the white tees, and women from the white, or more frequently, from the red tees.

The changing of the holes on the putting greens from flat to various undulating surfaces adds challenge and zest to the game. On many courses, especially those bordering the ocean or in the mountains, the ball may roll over the slanting surfaces in a direction exactly opposite the one decided on by the player. The story is told that after one man played an oceanside course for the first time, he became so frustrated trying to figure out the roll of the ball on the greens that he returned the next day with a carpenter's level to check the slopes of the putting greens. (The rules of golf do not permit the use of such a device.)

Courses having all relatively short holes (executive and par-3 courses) offer certain advantages to the novice. A simpler version of golf is played; thus, more success and pleasure are possible for beginners. For all players, these short courses are challenging, offer practice in the important short game, and require less time for the completion of a round.

Golf is not all of life, but to have the opportunity to play on outstandingly beautiful and ability-testing golf courses throughout the world is enriching life for an increasing number of people.

Golf Clubs

A player is permitted to carry a maximum of fourteen clubs to play golf. All golfers do not use a full set, and those using a full set do not all select the same clubs. However, the usual set of fourteen clubs consists of one putter, nine irons, and four woods. (See "Selection of Accessories and Equipment" in chapter 10.)

Putter

The putter has an almost vertical clubface and usually has a relatively short shaft. It is used principally on the putting green (and near the green) to stroke and roll the ball into the hole. The design and construction of putters vary greatly: The shaft may be attached to any part of the clubhead, the size and contour of the grip may be different from the standard grip of the woods and irons, and the clubhead may be made in a variety of shapes (fig. 1.3).

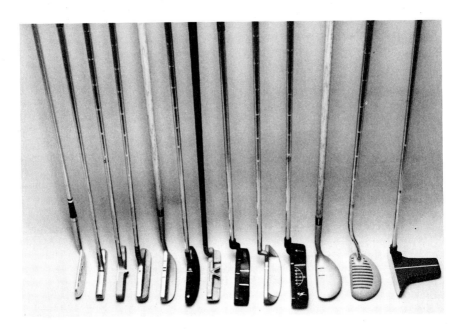

Figure 1.3
Putters—various head styles.

Irons

A matched set of irons consists of eight or nine clubs: The eight-club set in-cludes the 3-iron through 9-iron and wedge; the nine-club set includes the 2-iron through 9-iron and wedge (fig. 1.5). Due to the differences in shaft lengths and clubface lofts, the distances and trajectories of shots hit with the irons vary considerably (fig. 1.6). The distance differential between each of the irons is approximately 10 yards. For instance, if you can hit a ball 130 yards with a 5-iron, then you should be able to hit a ball 140 yards with a 4-iron and 120 yards with a 6-iron.

Wedges have heavier clubheads and greater lofts than 9-irons. Although these clubs are designated as pitching or sand wedges, both are used to hit shots either from the turf or the sand, depending on the player's preference.

Besides the wedges, other special irons are made for hitting the ball short distances. Irons with medium loft and relatively short shafts are used to play low trajectory shots (run-up or chip shots) to the putting green. These clubs are marketed under various names but are generally called chipping irons.

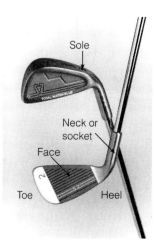

Figure 1.4
Parts of a clubhead. Courtesy
of Square Two Golf Company.

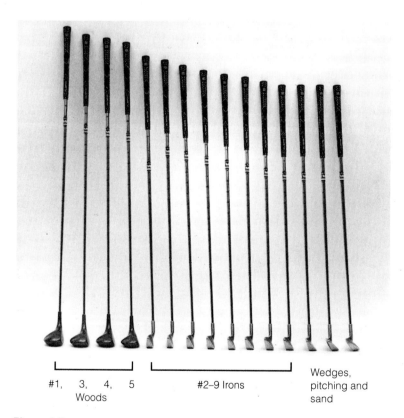

#1,   3,   4,   5   #2–9 Irons   Wedges,
     Woods   pitching and
                                              sand

Figure 1.5
Woods and irons. Courtesy of Square Two Golf Company.

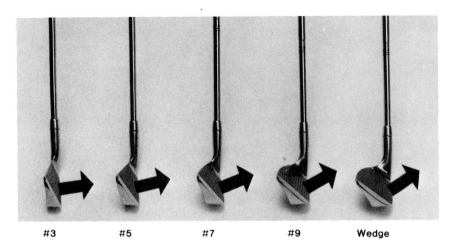

| #3 | #5 | #7 | #9 | Wedge |

Figure 1.6
Clubface loft—irons. Courtesy of Cobra Golf Company.

In the past, irons were referred to by name. For example, a 2-iron was known as a mid-iron, a 5-iron was called a mashie, and a 9-iron was known as a niblick. Today, you seldom hear any numbered iron called by name.

Woods

Matched sets of woods are usually made up of four clubs, numbers 1, 3, 4, and 5 (fig. 1.7). Formerly, the 2-wood was included in all sets, but its limited usefulness caused it to decline in popularity. The shafts of the woods are longer than those of the irons, so that you can expect to hit the ball farther with these clubs than with the irons (fig. 1.8). Like the irons, the different-numbered woods vary in shaft length and clubface loft. The almost vertical face of the 1-wood, the driver, usually restricts its use to hitting the ball from a tee. The distance differential is approximately 10 yards between each of the different-numbered woods.

Wood clubs with greater lofts than the 5-wood are gaining in favor. Some players prefer to use these clubs in place of the long irons. Distinct changes have been made in the materials used for the clubheads of woods. Besides being made of wood, the clubheads are also made of such materials as stainless steel and graphite. For want of a better name, they are called metal woods and graphite woods.

For Review

1. How important is the mental side of the game to the advanced player, the average player, and the novice? What part does the subconscious play in executing a golf shot?

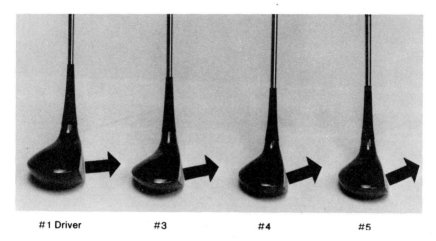

| #1 Driver | #3 | #4 | #5 |

Figure 1.7
Clubface loft—woods. Courtesy of Cobra Golf Company.

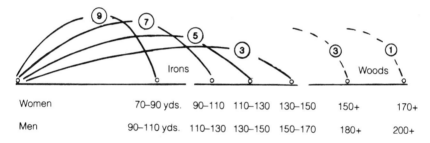

| Women | 70–90 yds. | 90–110 | 110–130 | 130–150 | 150+ | 170+ |
| Men | 90–110 yds. | 110–130 | 130–150 | 150–170 | 180+ | 200+ |

Figure 1.8
Range of approximate distances for average golfers.

2. If a player can consistently hit the ball 150 yards with a 5-iron, what club is this player apt to choose for a shot of 110 yards?
3. How is par determined for a hole? Why can a given hole on the course you play regularly present different challenges from time to time?

Safety—An Important Lesson

2

Golf is a relatively safe game, but if accidents occur, they can be serious. Most accidents happen because players are careless or uninformed about safety practices. You have a *responsibility* for your safety and for the safety of others. Learn the rules that follow and *never take chances where safety is concerned.*

General Safety Rules

1. Follow all precautions given to you by your instructor.
2. Before you swing a wood or an iron club, make sure that no one is within range of your swing.
3. When another player is about to swing, be careful where you stand or walk. Stay well out of range of any swing.
4. Even though no one is within range of your swing, never swing carelessly so that the follow-through is directed toward anyone. You could hit and propel a pebble, rock, or divot toward that person. Also, although it is not likely to happen, the club could break or slip out of your hands.

Safety at the Practice Range

1. Stay in the designated tee area. Do not walk or step ahead of the tee line to retrieve tees or balls.
2. If someone is teaching you or you are coaching another player, stand opposite and facing that person. Never stand on the player's right or left side in the path of the club. (At a crowded driving range, be especially careful. The tee areas are set up for a single player; usually, the allotted space cannot accommodate both a student and a ''coach.'')

Safety on the Course

1. Do not stand or walk ahead of a player who is about to take a stroke that may endanger you. Similarly, before you are about to hit a ball, make certain that no one is standing or walking ahead of you.
2. Before playing any stroke, be sure that the group playing ahead is well out of range of your intended shot.

3. Before playing a shot to the putting green, wait until the group playing ahead has left the green and is safely out of range. When your group completes play on the putting green, replace the flagstick and leave the green immediately (see ''Etiquette—on the Putting Green'' in chapter 10).

4. If you hit a ball that is traveling toward someone and may endanger that person, immediately call ''Fore!'' loudly to alert the player. (This warning may enable the player to take cover or duck to protect the head and eyes.)

5. At par-3 holes on some courses, inviting the following foursome to tee off when all members of your group have played their shots to the putting green is an accepted practice. While this following group is teeing off, your foursome should stand off the back edge of the green, preferably to one side of the hole, and watch the oncoming shots. After the tee shots have been taken, your group can then proceed to putt out.

6. Upon reaching the putting green of any hole, place your golf clubs or cart on the side or back of the green nearest the next tee. *Never* place your clubs in front of the green. A player in the following group may carelessly shoot as you walk to the front of the green to retrieve your clubs, thereby putting you in a dangerous position, possibly in the direct line of a ball flying to the green.

7. If an object such as a tree or boulder is in your desired line of play, try to hit a safe shot avoiding the obstruction. Do not endanger yourself by hitting a ball that could rebound off the obstacle and fly back toward you. (If necessary, warn your playing companions to be alert or to take cover should your ball hit the object and ricochet.)

8. A golf course is extremely hazardous during lightning storms. Avoid playing during such storms.

Safe Use of a Motorized Cart

When using a motorized cart to ride around the course, drive with care and follow the course rules for operation of the vehicle:

1. No more than two people should occupy the cart, and only authorized players should operate it. Do not allow children to drive the vehicle.

2. Never step out of the cart while it is moving. Remain seated and keep arms, legs, and feet inside the cart until it comes to a full stop.

3. Drive slowly on slopes. Drive straight up and straight down hillsides.

4. Drive slowly when turning and avoid making sharp turns.

5. Be especially careful when driving on wet areas. To avoid skidding, drive slowly. Do not apply brakes suddenly.

6. Set the brakes before you leave the cart.

Many sports people carry personal liability insurance for protection in case of accidents. The protection offered by these policies may merit your investigation and consideration.

Make golf a safe game. Follow all safety precautions: *Be considerate, be alert,* and *use common sense.*

For Review

1. Name at least six safety precautions for driving or riding in a motorized cart on a golf course.
2. On a par-3 hole, your group has reached the putting green and has signaled players following to tee off. While waiting for their play, where should your group stand?
3. Why is it dangerous to swing so that the follow-through is directed toward a person even though the person is out of range of your swing?

Basic Golf Concepts

3

Too often, golfers want to know "how" to swing a golf club. They want to know the intricate details of the swing, the complex analysis of the movement. Even if such an analysis were possible, what then? A full golf swing takes about two seconds. In that time, how much can you think about and translate into action? Fortunately, conscious messages do not have to be sent to all involved body parts at the correct split second to make a golf swing. If this were necessary, no one could swing a golf club successfully.

Focusing on Details Can Slow Your Progress

Questions on whether the swing is natural or unnatural are meaningless. People of all ages, even those with physical handicaps, have learned to swing a golf club well. Some people have difficulty learning the golf swings, but the problem is not in the movement. Attempting to execute the "how" by performing many details of action is one of the chief causes of learning difficulties. Trying to think of and perform many parts of the swing in two seconds is impossible and frustrating.

Emphasizing even one detail while swinging may cause trouble. No one questions that the left arm should remain fairly straight during a swing (putting excepted). However, when the cue "straight left arm" is carried beyond easy extension to an incorrect *stiff* position, the motion of swinging is restricted. Overemphasizing any detail can become an error that limits or distorts the whole swing.

Trust Your Innate Ability for Coordination

Purpose is an important factor in determining the form of a motion. Suppose you wish to throw a ball straight up into the air. Your arm swings up sharply, and your weight shifts upward with the motion. This coordination occurs without thought. You neither think of swinging your arm up nor of shifting your weight upward. Rather, you think of throwing the ball straight up into the air— and you do it!

Concentrating on the objective of the golf stroke—striking the ball to a target by swinging the club in a circular pattern—can develop a good swing. Novices fear that they cannot learn all the details of the swing. A player asks: "How can I remember to do all those things?" The encouraging answer, of course, is that thinking of numerous details is unnecessary. Trust your body to supply and coordinate many particulars. The everyday motor skills you perform are evidence that this wonderful talent for coordination works almost automatically.

Basic Swing Concepts

Understanding certain mechanical principles of clubhead action is important. Yet, many players ignore such information. Instead of directing their attention to the clubhead, they focus on what to do with some body part: head, shoulder, hip, knee, ad infinitum. If a ball is hit poorly, they may work on changing the movement of some body part, rather than examining the trouble source—clubface and ball contact. Simple concepts of *swing pattern, clubface and ball contact,* and *clubhead speed and distance* provide guideposts for swinging a golf club well and hitting good golf shots.

Swing Pattern

A correct mental image of the golf swing is fundamental. To register the total concept of the arc, the full golf swing must be viewed from the front and the side. The swing is a circular motion on an inclined plane. While the clubhead gradually travels upward, it also travels around the body. The swing is three-dimensional. The swing to strike the ball a shorter distance varies from the full swing in length only. The distinguishing plane of the arc is less evident in the smaller swings made with shorter clubs (fig. 3.1).

The clubhead follows a path of least resistance. The arc described by the clubhead may be a normal outcome of swinging the club to strike the ball from the ground to a distant target.

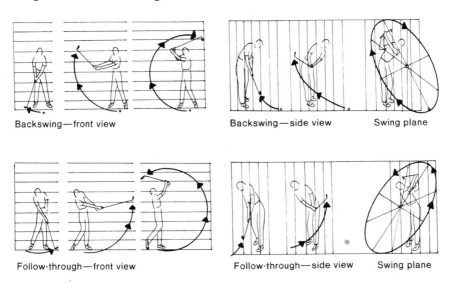

Backswing—front view   Backswing—side view   Swing plane

Follow-through—front view   Follow-through—side view   Swing plane

Figure 3.1
Swing arc.

Figure 3.2
Clubhead path close to ground.

Inside   On target line   Inside

Figure 3.3
Clubhead path through ball impact.

Along with the total swing concept, correct images of how the clubhead should travel through the impact zone are important:

1. With relation to ground level, *the clubhead travels close to the grass before and after ball contact* (fig. 3.2).
2. With relation to the intended line of flight, *the clubhead enters the contact area from inside the line of flight, travels on the line of flight, and on the follow-through, travels inside the intended line of ball flight.* This is a result of the clubhead traveling in an arc around you (fig. 3.3).

Clubface and Ball Contact

The flight and directional path of the ball can be directly related only to the contact of the clubface with the ball. Other factors may affect this contact, but in themselves, they do not propel the ball—only the clubface can do that.

When a ball is hit properly, the slant (loft) of the clubface determines the ball's upward flight. A struggling golfer may say: "I can't get the ball up," or "I can't get under the ball." Until this player stops trying to hit the ball up into the air, his or her troubles will continue and probably increase. Do not try to propel the ball upward. This understanding is basic to hitting good golf shots: *The clubface—not an effort on your part—will loft the ball into the air* (fig. 3.4).

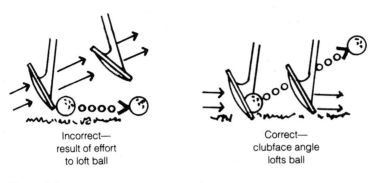

Incorrect—
result of effort
to loft ball

Correct—
clubface angle
lofts ball

Figure 3.4
Ball contact.

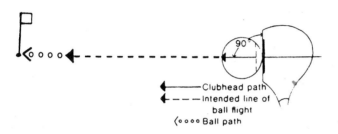

Clubhead path
Intended line of
ball flight
⟨∘∘∘∘ Ball path

Figure 3.5
Impact producing straight shot to target.

The factors that determine the direction the ball will travel are the clubhead path through impact and the clubface position with relation to the clubhead path. *If at ball contact the clubhead is traveling on the intended line of flight, and if the clubface is at right angles to that line, the ball will travel straight along the intended path to the target* (fig. 3.5).

Golf requires a high degree of accuracy. A small error in clubface and ball contact may cause a great error in shot result. Considering the size of the golf ball and the small hitting surface of the clubface, it is a wonder that so many fine golf shots are made.

Clubhead Speed and Distance

One distinguishing characteristic of a fine golf swing is the smooth, flowing acceleration of the clubhead. Many players neglect to drill on this quality of the swing, but not the expert golfers. The experts "tune" their swings to smoothness, ease, tempo, and rhythm. Their objective is to develop one swing that they can trust to repeat *and repeat*. This one smooth, accelerating swing produces great speed and distance—sometimes, a greater distance than the player expected. This is a surprising and pleasant happening, especially when a long tee shot is desired. But it is a "happening," and wise players know this. Their practice has paid off and will continue to do so. They are on the right track.

Experimentation is the downfall of many players in their quest for long-distance shots. They simply never get down to working on one swing and trusting that swing. Their swings are in a continual state of flux. These players would do well to follow the practices of fine golfers: to have the patience to work on developing one well-timed swinging motion; and to *permit*, not force, clubhead speed, and thus distance, to develop.

A typical mistake many players make is trying to swing faster or "harder" with certain clubs. For instance, after practice in hitting 7-iron shots, a player changes to hitting 5-iron shots. Knowing that the ball should travel about 20 yards farther, a player may instinctively try to "add something" to the swing to get more distance. This is a mistake. The longer club, with less clubface loft, will produce the added distance.

Through intelligent practice, you learn what the optimum speed is for swinging a golf club. The timing and smooth blending of forces that come with correct muscular action, together with the size of the arc, produce clubhead speed and distance, with accuracy.

Learning by Imitation

Imitation can be either an aid or a hindrance to learning. Young people imitate easily and to a high degree. Unlike some adults, they do not imitate on the intellectual or analytical level, but rather on a "subconscious" level. They grasp the *movement as a whole*. Pictures and feelings are registered, but not in words. Many caddies and young people have imitated fine golf swings, and this has played a part in their becoming good golfers. But when players try to copy minor swing details, swing styles, mannerisms, or idiosyncracies, they usually end up with what they copied—worthless details, not a better golf stroke.

In your imaginative brain center, you probably have a picture of a golf swing, accompanied by a feeling for the stroke. This may be a copy of one swing or an impression that has evolved from seeing many golf swings. If the picture is of a whole swing in good form, and the feeling is one of ease and good timing, then this mental image can be an aid in swinging the golf club well.

Progression in Learning the Swings

Skillful golfers prepare to play a round of golf by starting their practice with the medium or short irons. They hit shots requiring less than the full swing and then work to the longer swings and the longer clubs. This makes sense. The short swing is an important stroke of the game. The feel and touch for all golf swings are best found and recovered in these short strokes. Short swings also serve as easy muscle and joint warm-ups for the full swing.

Ayako Okamoto, Member, Advisory Staff, Mizuno Golf Company.

The foregoing statements suggest that, *if* it is best to start learning golf with a particular swing, then the choice should be the small swing. The beginner need not delay working on the longer swings, but patience is recommended. You will achieve more success in striking the ball with the less complex short swing than with the full swing. Success in striking the ball makes learning and practice more enjoyable, as well as more effective. The putting stroke can be learned and practiced right along with the other strokes.

The Real Secret to Learning Golf

Useful guides can be given for learning golf and executing the swings, but no exact formula can be proposed. Who can confidently say that he or she has all the answers to learning golf or to hitting fine golf shots consistently? Novices watch champions, note a detail of the swing, and think they have "discovered the secret" of good golf. Of one thing you can be sure—the champion does not want to know this *secret!* The champion already knows the **real secret:** *following the fundamentals of good form in the grip, stance, and swing, and hitting thousands of golf balls in practice and play.*

You will become proficient in swinging a golf club as you have become proficient in other motor skills—through repetition. Through trial and error, and through trial and success, you will discard unsuccessful swing actions and record successful swings in your "muscle memory" and in your subconscious. You can develop an effective golf swing only by following the basics of good form and by swinging a golf club many times.

For Review

1. Why is the development of and reliance on *one* swing important?
2. How will concentrating on various details of the stroke affect your swing and your golf shots?
3. Describe the correct clubhead path—before, at, and after impact—in relation to the ground level and the intended line of ball flight.
4. What are the advantages in starting practice with short swings before progressing to full swings?

Addressing the Ball

4

Taking the correct grip and the proper stance are essential preliminary steps in executing successful golf shots with the irons and woods. Some shots may be hit well when the fundamentals of grip and stance appear to be defied. Neglect of the fundamentals, however, only serves to tear apart a swing because compensations must be made *constantly* to counteract the incorrect positions. Your best chance of developing a sound swing and game is to *start with the correct grip and stance.*

The Grip

Types of Grips

The *overlapping grip* is most widely used. In this grip, the little finger of the right hand rests on or overlaps the index finger of the left hand. In the *interlocking grip,* the little finger of the right hand and the index finger of the left hand interlock. An advantage of both of these positions is the feeling of unity between the hands because of the overlapping or interlocking of the fingers. An additional advantage claimed for the overlapping grip is that both index fingers are on the shaft. Index fingers and thumbs are key components in holding anything. A person with small hands may prefer the interlocking grip. The person who lacks strength or who has small hands may find the *ten-finger grip* most suitable. (See fig. 4.1.)

Overlapping   Interlocking   Ten-finger

Figure 4.1
Types of grips.

The three grip positions are much alike: The only difference among them is the placement of the little finger of the right hand and the index finger of the left hand. All three grips have been used successfully. However, most golfers favor the overlapping grip. Individual preference, feel, strength, and size of hands may all be factors in choosing the best grip for you.

Steps in Taking the Grip

As an additional aid for learning the correct grip, see instructions for use of Grip-Guide pattern, pages 34–37.

Left Hand

1. Place the club sole flat on the ground and support the tip of the handle with your right hand.
2. Let your left arm hang at your side. Feel the easy hanging position of the left hand and arm.

Figure 4.2
Left-hand grip—step 1.

Figure 4.3
Left-hand grip—step 2.

3. Without changing the natural hanging position of the left hand, move it forward to the club so that the club handle extends across the middle section of the index finger and back across the palm near the base of the little finger (fig. 4.2). The hand, arm, and shoulder should still be in an easy, relaxed position. The back of the left hand faces the direction of the intended target. (Avoid the common error of gripping "under" the handle with the palm facing skyward.)
4. Keeping the left hand in this proper position and relaxed, close the fingers and take hold of the club handle (fig. 4.3). Hold the club with some firmness but without tension. Holding the club with the left hand, you should be able to move the clubhead easily. (Try moving the clubhead just a few inches back and forth on the ground while maintaining this correct grip.)

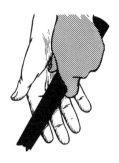

Figure 4.4
Right-hand grip—step 1.

Figure 4.5
Right-hand grip—step 2.

Figure 4.6
Left-hand grip—checkpoints.

Right Hand

1. Let the right arm hang easily at your side. Note its natural hanging position.
2. Without changing the easy hanging position of the right hand, move the hand to the club so that the club handle lies across the middle part of the index finger. The lifeline of the right palm is superimposed over the left thumb (fig. 4.4). The palm of the right hand faces the direction of the intended target. The palms of the hands face each other. The right hand, arm, and shoulder should still be in an easy position.
3. Close the fingers and palm of the right hand and take hold of the club (fig. 4.5). In taking the overlapping grip, allow the little finger of the right hand to fall naturally over the index finger of the left hand. For the interlocking position, raise the index finger of the left hand and interlock it with the little finger of the right hand. The hand positions should not change when the fingers are overlapped or interlocked.
4. Check the face of the club to see that it is *square* to the intended line of ball flight. (Check the firmness of the grip and ease of motion by moving the clubhead a few inches back and forth along the ground.)

Checkpoints—Left Hand

Take hold of the club, look down at your grip, and check the following numbered points with figure 4.6:

1. The V formed by the thumb and index finger points to the general area between the chin and the right shoulder. Checking where the V points is a matter of judgment. Follow your instructor's specific instructions.
2. The base segment of the thumb touches the side of the hand, forming a line.
3. The left thumb is slightly to the right of a center line along the shaft.

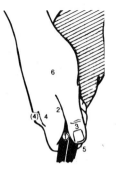

Figure 4.7
Complete grip—checkpoints for right hand.

ıuckles at the base of the first two fingers, and perhaps also the
ɘ at the base of the third finger, can be seen.
5. The tip of the thumb and the tip of the index finger lie close to each other.

Checkpoints—Right Hand

Check the following numbered points with figure 4.7:

1. The V formed by the thumb and index finger points to the general area between the chin and right shoulder.
2. The base segment of the thumb touches the side of the hand, forming a line.
3. The right thumb is placed slightly to the left of a center line along the shaft.
4. The knuckle at the base of the index finger, and perhaps also the knuckle at the base of the long finger, can be seen.
5. The tip of the thumb and the tip of the index finger lie close to each other. (The tip of the thumb does not extend down the shaft beyond the middle segment of the index finger.)
6. The left thumb fits in the lifeline of the right palm.

Hand Coordination

The hands send and receive messages about the swing. They are the sensory controls. They coordinate. In an effective hold on the club, they feel like a single unit working together, neither one overpowering the other. The left-hand grip is more of a finger and palm grip, while the right is mainly a finger grip. The club must be held with authority, but this authority is for swinging the club, not for crushing the shaft! A vise-like, tenacious grip usually radiates tension up through the forearms, arms, and shoulders, thus preventing a free swing. The hold on the club must be firm, yet with a degree of ease and comfort, and must remain that way throughout the swing.

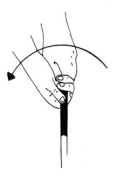

Grip favoring shot
to left

Grip favoring shot
to right

Figure 4.8
Hand positions affecting shot direction.

Some players believe that wearing a glove on the left hand or gloves on both hands gives them a better feeling of holding the club. (Wearing gloves may provide some protection for the fingers and hands. Players unaccustomed to swinging a club or engaged in extensive practice tend to develop sore hands and blisters.)

Relation of Hand Position to Directional Ball Flight

The position of the hands on the club affects the directional flight of the ball. For instance, if the right hand is placed on the club so that the palm points skyward, the ball is likely to travel to the left of the target. The reason for this can be easily demonstrated. Grip the club with the right hand with the palm facing skyward and the clubface square to the intended target. Keeping the same hold on the club, turn the right hand so that the palm faces the intended line of ball flight. Note that the clubface turns over and is in a closed position pointing to the left and downward. If either or both hands are placed on the club contrary to the easy hanging position, there is a tendency for the hand or hands to return to the natural position during the swing, thereby changing the clubface alignment at impact (fig. 4.8). Hand position does not always determine the directional flight of the ball because various compensations made during the swing may affect the clubface position.

Changing the grip to alter the ball flight is for the advanced player. When the hands are shifted to the left, the shot is likely to travel right; a shift of the hands to the right is likely to cause the ball to travel to the left. Changing the grip from the correct to the incorrect to eliminate errors in ball flight is not recommended. A balanced grip, as though "shaking hands" with the club handle and with the palms in opposition to each other, is basic for correctly holding the club (fig. 4.8).

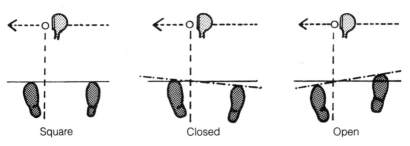

Square   Closed   Open

Figure 4.9
Types of stances.

The Stance

Types of Stances

Stances are classified by drawing a relationship between the intended line of ball direction and an imaginary line extending across the front edge of the toes (fig. 4.9). These two lines are parallel in the *square stance,* the one most widely used. This stance, with the lines across the toes, hips, and shoulders parallel to the target line, is a natural position to assume.

If the stance is changed to an *open* or *closed* one for certain shots, the change should be slight. A square stance is recommended for most golf shots.

Stances vary in width for a logical reason: The width of the stance should fit the purpose of the swing. To hit a ball a long distance, the feet are placed approximately shoulder width apart. This stance allows you to swing the club in a wide arc and to keep your balance while swinging the clubhead swiftly. To hit the ball a short distance, take a narrow stance. The same principle applies to the distance you stand from the ball. For distance shots, using the longer-shafted clubs, you will necessarily stand farther from the ball than for shorter distance shots.

Steps in Taking the Stance

1. Sight and draw an imaginary line through the ball to the target.
2. Visualize the desired shot.
3. Holding the club correctly, place the club sole flat on the ground back of the ball as you sight again to see that the clubface is pointing toward the target. The edge of the clubhead where the sole and face meet should be perpendicular to the intended line of ball flight (Step 1 in figs. 4.10, 4.11). The proper distance from the ball is established when the clubhead is placed back of the ball. The easily extended arms and the length of the shaft determine this distance. Avoid crowding the ball or stretching to reach it.

Step 1   Step 2

Figure 4.10
Taking stance for short approach shot.

Step 1   Step 2

Figure 4.11
Taking stance for wood shot (Michael Hemphill).

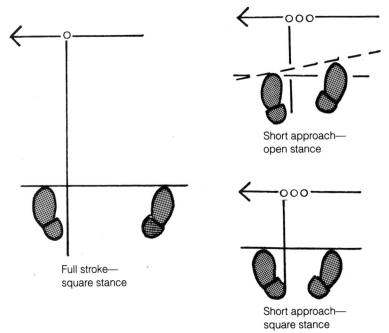

Figure 4.12
Stance and ball position relationship.

4. Move the feet into the proper stance (Step 2 in figs. 4.10, 4.11).
   —For the short approach shot, take a comfortable, narrow stance. A slightly open stance may be preferred over the square stance.
   —For long shots, take a comfortable stance with the feet about shoulder width apart.

Relation of Stance to Ball Position

The position of the ball in relation to the feet may vary slightly. For most long shots, the unanimous recommendation is to play the ball approximately opposite a point inside the left heel. For shorter shots, the ball may be played from near this spot to a point extending toward the center of the stance (fig. 4.12).

Checkpoints—The Stance

1. The left arm and club shaft are approximately in a straight line. The arms hang easily from the shoulders—they are not held stiff. The right shoulder is naturally slightly lower than the left because the right hand is placed lower on the grip.

Figure 4.13
Addressing the ball (Doreen La Donna and Michael Hemphill).

2. The hands may be either slightly ahead of or above the ball. When you look down on the hands, it may appear that they are in a position left of the clubhead.
3. The toes are turned out slightly. Turning the left foot out slightly more than the right may afford a freer swing through the ball. The knees are slightly bent, "easy" and ready to move.
4. The body is bent slightly forward from the hip joints, and the back is fairly straight, but not rigid.
5. In the square stance, the imaginary lines running across the shoulders, hips, and front tips of the shoes are parallel to the intended line of flight.
6. For long shots, the feet are about shoulder width apart, and the ball is opposite a point inside of the left heel. For short shots, the stance is narrow, and the ball is opposite a point extending from the inside of the left heel toward the center of the stance.

Make the steps in addressing the ball simple and concise (figs. 4.10, 4.11, 4.13). When you know how to hold the club properly and how to take the correct stance, avoid making a "production" of addressing the ball. The simpler the process the better. You can trust your senses to aim correctly and to settle in a stance that is good for you.

The Waggle and Forward Press

A waggle is a movement of the *clubhead* in preparation for swinging the club—a rehearsal for starting the backswing. After the stance is taken, the clubhead is moved away from the ball a short distance in the correct backswing path. Then it is moved forward to the ball and back to the address position. This gives you a "feel" of the club and a sense of ease and confidence for starting the swing. The action of picking the club up and setting it down is not a waggle. Avoid such nervous actions.

A forward press is a movement of the body in preparation for beginning the swing. Just before the swing is started, there is a slight "rocking" of weight to the left leg, accompanied by a slight bend of the right knee toward the left: hence, the name of the action—a press forward. Some golfers find that this slight shift forward helps them to start the swing. Other players of varying skill do not use a forward press, or if they do, the movement is so subtle that it can scarcely be seen.

The waggle and the forward press are not necessary actions but, rather, auxiliary ones.

Practice Suggestions

- Practice taking the grip. Place your hands on the club, check the grip, then release your hold on the club. Repeat this action until the correct grip becomes routine. By applying the checkpoints and using the Grip-Guide (fig 4.16), you can be confident that you will take and maintain a correct hold on the club. It is easier to make any necessary adjustments to the grip if first you take an easy, instead of a firm, hold on the club. Firm up the grip only after making sure it is correct.

- In your early practice in taking the grip, follow the steps in the text: Place the left hand on the club and check the hand position; then place the right hand on the club and check the complete grip. The grip will become comfortable and easy with practice. After practice in taking the grip in two steps, take the grip almost simultaneously with both hands. Have a feeling of the hands fitting together on the handle so that they can work as a unit in swinging the club.

- Holding the club correctly, practice moving the clubhead in various patterns, such as circles and figure eights. These exercises test the grip in action. The wrists and arms must be relaxed and flexible while the correct hold on the club is maintained. Note that, as you focus on moving the clubhead, the wrists and arms move—a responsive action.

- Some simple exercises can help you to develop grip and arm strength: Squeeze a soft sponge ball or towel; flex and extend the fingers and arms, offering your own resistance. Strength is developed by gradually increasing the number of movements you can make in a given amount of time.

- Address the ball and check the address position. As you do so, "let go," especially through the shoulders, so that you are relaxed and ready to move. Maintain a correct and firm grip.

- Practice taking the stance to different targets. Check to see whether the stance is square by laying a club on the ground with the shaft touching the front tips of your shoes. Then step back of the ball and see whether the club shaft is parallel to the intended line of flight (fig. 4.14).

- Practice maintaining the correct body posture during the swing with the following simple exercise: Without holding a club, assume an easy, comfortable stance. Check that feet are shoulder width apart, knees are "easy," and arms are hanging free of the body. Swing the arms back and forth. Watch a spot on the ground to maintain a fairly steady head position. Let the body and legs "give" with the swing. Gradually increase the arm swing to a point where the shoulders alternately move under the chin. Maintain the feel of the correct body posture throughout the swing.

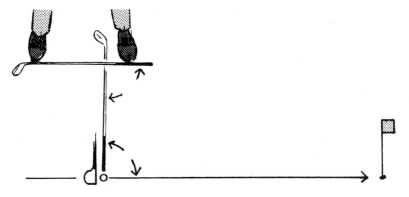

Figure 4.14
Checking alignment with golf clubs.

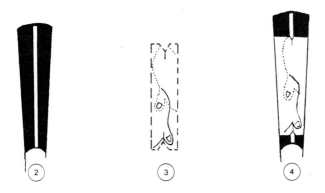

Figure 4.15
Placing Grip-Guide pattern on club handle.

Grip-Guide

How to Place Grip-Guide Pattern (4.16) on Club Handle

Refer to figure 4.15 for circled numbers ②, ③, and ④.

1. Set the sole of a medium iron flat on the ground, clubface pointing to the target.
② Mark a line down the center front of the club grip.
③ Copy or cut out the rectangular form of the Grip-Guide (fig. 4.16).
④ Place the notches of the Grip-Guide on the center line of the club handle and tape onto the club.

As an alternative to placing the Grip-Guide on a golf club, make a simple practice device by rolling up newspaper sheets to the approximate circumference and length of the grip portion of a club. Secure with tape. Attach a copy of the Grip-Guide to the roll of paper.

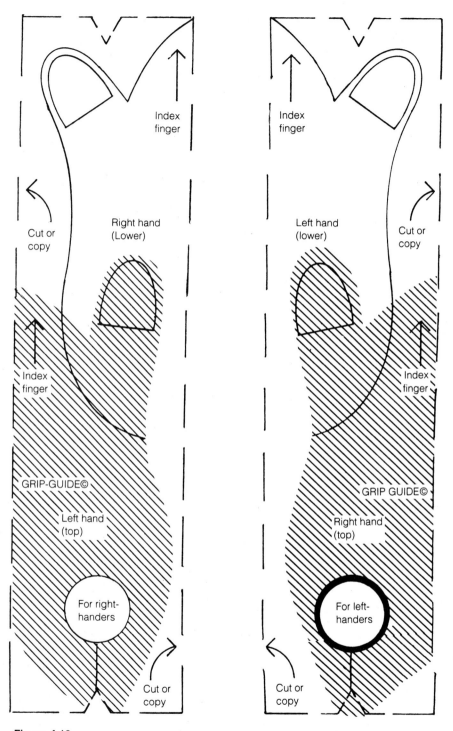

Figure 4.16
Grip-Guide.

How to Place Hands on Grip-Guide Pattern

The key to the correct hold on the club is placing the thumb and index finger of each hand on the pattern. With the positions of the thumbs and index fingers correct, the remaining fingers, as they are wrapped around the handle, normally assume their proper positions.

Top Hand

Place the thumb and index finger on the pattern and take hold of the club. The edge of the index finger should fall on or near the line indicated, forming a V between the thumb and index finger.

Checkpoints for top hand:

1. The thumb is slightly to the side of the center line.
2. The V between the thumb and index finger points in the general direction of the right shoulder (left-handers: left shoulder).
3. As you look down on the grip, the knuckles at the base of the first two fingers (and possibly the third finger) can be seen.
4. The tip of the thumb and the lower edge of the index finger are in a position approximately equidistant down the club handle.

Lower Hand

Place the thumb and index finger in position on the pattern. Wrap all of the fingers, except the little finger, around the handle. For the overlapping grip, let the little finger overlap the index finger of the top hand; for the interlocking grip, interlock the little finger and the index finger of the top hand; for the ten-finger grip, wrap the little finger with the others around the club.

Checkpoints for lower hand:

1. The thumb is slightly to the side of the center line.
2. The V between the thumb and index finger points in the general direction of the right shoulder (left-handers: left shoulder).
3. As you look down on the grip, the knuckle at the base of the index finger (and possibly the long finger) can be seen.
4. The tip of the thumb and the lower edge of the index finger are in a position approximately equidistant down the handle.
5. The palms of the hands face each other.

Adjustments

For extremely large or small hands, place the thumbs and index fingers in the same relative position that the Grip-Guide indicates, but outside or inside the guidelines. In most cases, little or no adjustment is necessary.

After placing the hands on the Grip-Guide in their proper positions, slight adjustments may be made for greater ease in holding the club, but do not fail to keep the thumbs and index fingers close to the pattern.

Using the Grip-Guide

After the Grip-Guide is taped firmly in place, practice taking the grip. When you feel that you are holding the club securely and that there is no danger of the club slipping out of your hands, practice taking small swings and progress to longer swings.

The Grip-Guide should help you to learn the correct grip. When you feel confident that you can hold the club properly, discontinue using the guide. It has then served its purpose.

For Review

1. In which direction is the ball likely to travel in relation to the target if the correct grip is altered by a shift of the hands to the right or to the left, or by the right-hand palm facing skyward?
2. What purposes are served by the waggle and the forward press? How important is it that these actions be performed prior to the club swing?
3. When you take a square stance, what imaginary lines should be parallel to the intended line of flight?
4. Even though it is possible to hit good shots despite faults in the grip and stance, why is it important to make sure that these positions are correct?
5. How does the position of addressing the ball differ for an 8-iron, a 5-iron, and a 1-wood?

Short Approach Shots

5

The short approach shots played to the putting green are chip (run-up) shots and pitch shots. The chip shot is usually played with a medium iron. The ball travels in a relatively low trajectory. The chip shot will, after landing, roll a longer distance than a typical pitch shot, due to the lack of backspin and to the low trajectory.

The pitch shot is played with a high-lofted iron; thus, the ball travels in a high trajectory and, upon landing, tends to stop with little or no forward roll. When a ball is contacted squarely with a lofted iron, the clubface compresses the ball below its center of gravity, thus imparting backspin to it. This backspin plus the height from which the ball falls to the ground tend to stop the ball's forward motion when it lands. In some instances, the ball bounces backward upon landing.

Approach shots vary greatly in length, from perhaps 20 feet or less to about 100 yards. These strokes plus the putting stroke—the *short game*—make up a substantial percentage of a player's shots in a round of golf.

The terms *one-quarter, one-half,* and *three-quarter* are often used to describe the approximate lengths of the swings. Through practice, you learn how far to swing the club to hit the ball a given distance. After sighting and judging the distance for a shot, through the remarkable sense of feel (kinesthetic sense), you swing the club the length your eye, feel, and experience dictate. Subconsciously, the synthesis of the judgments translates into the execution of the shot. At times, all golfers experience the thrill of stroking approach shots expertly, either by having the ball come to rest inches from the hole or by holing the shot.

A Look at the Swings

The very short approach swing may be thought of as a simple motion of "sweeping" the club back and through. In this pendulum-like motion, you swing the clubhead close to the ground and on or close to the intended target line (fig. 5.1, see also fig. 3.2). A smooth, swinging motion results in a consistent and correct clubhead path:

- Swing the clubhead in an arc, keeping the same radius throughout the stroke. Thus, the arms maintain the easy, extended position they assumed in addressing the ball.

Figure 5.1
Clubhead path—pendulum-like swing

Figure 5.2
Approximate one-quarter swing.

- If the shoulders and arms lack tension, they will react, thus cooperating with the hands and clubhead swing.
- Little or no action of the wrists or other body parts occurs.

As your distance objective increases, increase the length of the swing accordingly (figs. 5.2 and 5.3). The longer swing is not a new swing: it is a continuation of the smaller one.

In swinging a golf club to stroke the ball longer distances, responsive and correct movements may occur—what a simple and effective way of learning! Avoid *detailed* analysis. Consider the following actions and responses:

Figure 5.3
Half swing.

- The clubhead path is close to the ground and on the target line through the impact zone. As the swing lengthens, the clubhead naturally moves upward on a path inside the intended target line on the back and forward swings (see fig. 3.3).
- With a correct grip, not a tense one, the wrists bend gradually on the backswing. This action increases as the swing lengthens. No conscious effort should be made to ''use'' the wrists.
- The easily extended left arm maintains the radius of the swing, while the right arm, in accommodation, bends slightly in the backswing.
- If the stance is comfortable and the knees are bent slightly, the body may ''give'' in the direction of the swing. As the club is swung back, the left knee naturally ''gives'' to the right side, with a slight weight shift to the right. On the forward swing, the opposite action occurs.
- Emphasis throughout the stroke should be on swinging the clubhead. The longer swings produce more clubhead speed, thus distance. At impact, no extra effort should be made to *hit* the ball.

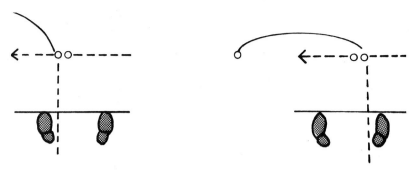

Figure 5.4
Ball position affecting height of ball flight.

Stroke Execution—Some Analysis and Detail

Good form can develop by swinging the clubhead. Many details of the swing can fuse into one unit—one that yields good golf shots.

Stance and Ball Position

For accuracy and for the feel and touch for stroking the ball a short distance, grip down ("choke up") on the handle and take a narrow, comfortable stance with the knees bent easily. Some players prefer to take a slightly open stance with slightly more weight carried to the left side. They believe that these adjustments help to establish a feel for a small swing. Also, they feel that the open stance allows a better view of the target. Whether the stance is square or slightly open, it must be comfortable and easy.

For approach shots, pinpointing an exact spot where the ball should be played in relation to the stance is difficult. In certain approach shots, some players prefer to play the ball opposite a point near the right foot. Through practice and experience, you will find the ideal position for stroking the ball, which will probably be in the area opposite the center of the stance and extending to a point opposite the inside of the left foot.

Sometimes, you may want to hit a ball in a higher or lower trajectory than normal for a specific club. A change in the position from which the ball is played may alter the ball's flight. A ball played more toward the left side of the stance tends to travel in a higher trajectory; one played more toward the right side tends to travel in a lower trajectory (fig. 5.4).

Grip, Hand Action, and Wrist Action

Changing the hold on the club during the swing almost always results in an awkward action of the hands and wrists. The positions of the hands can be checked at any point in the swing. Swing the club to a point where you wish to look at the grip; then stop the swing. Turn your head so that you are looking at the hands from the same angle as you observed them in addressing the ball. The grip should be the same as at address.

Incorrect—hands working against each other

Correct—hands working together

Figure 5.5
Hand action through ball impact.

Figure 5.6
Wrist action exercise.

A common fault in making the swing for the short approach shot is attempting to scoop the ball up into the air. In this erroneous action, the hands, instead of working together, work in opposition to each other. Near ball impact, the right hand moves forward and under, as the left hand holds back. A common outcome of this error is striking the ground with the clubhead before striking the ball. Through the impact area, both hands must move with the clubhead. At times, the hands may seem to be leading the clubhead (fig. 5.5).

The correct wrist motion, ranging from the slight movement of the small swing to the complete "cocking" of the wrists for the full swing, can be easily checked and rehearsed. Keeping the arms extended as in the address position, raise the clubhead and point it forward and then over your right shoulder (fig. 5.6). When

Figure 5.7
Leg, knee, and foot action exercise.

pointing the clubhead over the shoulder, keep the left elbow easily extended and let the right elbow bend. Note that, if the club handle is lifted with the hands and arms, there is no bending of the wrists.

Leg, Knee, and Foot Action

Action of the legs, knees, and feet is a part of swinging the clubhead in a certain direction. Because of previously developed muscle habits and tension, development of this combined action may require practice. This part of the swing can be practiced by itself without breaking up the blending action of all parts of the swing.

A simple practice exercise is to alternate bending the left knee toward a spot in front of the right foot, and then bending the right knee so that it points to a spot in front of the left foot. Accompanying this knee bending is some inward action of the ankle and foot. The weight shifts to the inner border of the foot and big toe. The heel may rise slightly from the ground, with the inner border rising less than the outer border (fig. 5.7). When your muscles have been trained to move in this manner and have developed a "feeling" for the motion, then you can expect to move the legs and feet correctly when you swing the club. This practice exercise, plus the directional influence of the swing, help to develop a correct and natural action—from the slight (almost subtle) movement in the shorter swings to the greater movement in the longer swings.

Head Position

In all golf swings, the head remains in a fairly stationary position until after the ball is struck. After ball contact, the head turns naturally to accommodate the follow-through of the swing. This is a mechanical aspect of the swing.

The cue "watch the ball until you strike it" is useful for maintaining a steady head position during the swing. But the cue "keep your head down" can cause serious errors if the position is exaggerated. If the head is held "down" so that the chin is resting on or near the chest, the shoulders are prevented from alternately moving under the chin on the backswing and follow-through. Even though this incorrect head position may not be a problem on very short swings with limited shoulder action, it is a habit to be avoided.

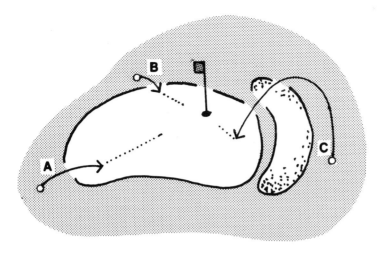

Figure 5.8
Approach shots.

One other error that may result from the "head down" cue is moving the head down and lower during the backswing. This restricts the backswing. Also, because the head must be moved back up to the address position when the ball is struck, the control and momentum of the clubhead are destroyed.

Selecting the Best Approach Shot

When a ball lies close to the putting green, the best stroke to play may be putting the ball over the apron and onto the putting surface. If the area between the ball and the edge of the green is relatively smooth and the ball will roll easily over the grass, choose to putt the ball rather than play a chip shot. Using a putter from off the putting green (sometimes humorously referred to as a "Texas wedge") can save strokes.

Chip Shot

Consider the following situations for playing a chip shot: One ball lies 50 feet from the hole and about 5 feet off the putting green; the other lies 20 feet from the hole and 3 feet off the putting surface (fig. 5.8 A,B). The fringe grass is heavy; therefore, rolling a putt through the area is questionable. The better shot, under these conditions, is a chip shot. The ball is played to carry over the heavy apron grass, land on the green, and roll toward the hole. For the longer shot, any of the medium irons—4-iron through 7-iron—is suitable. The best club to use for the shorter distance, where a limited roll is necessary after the ball lands on the green, is a high-lofted iron.

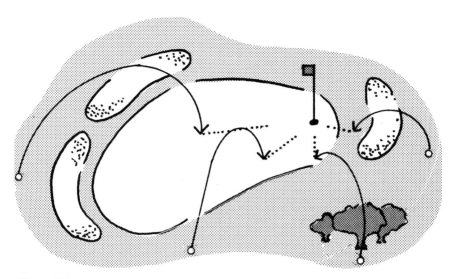

Figure 5.9
Pitch shots.

Pitch Shot

A typical short-distance pitch shot situation is one in which the ball lies about 30 to 40 yards from the hole and a deep bunker intervenes between the ball and the green (figs. 5.8C, 5.9). The ball must be stroked with a high-lofted iron, such as a wedge or 9-iron, so that it will carry over the bunker, land on the green, and have relatively little forward roll. The stroke for the pitch shot is a swinging motion as it is for the chip shot. A smooth, even swing can be "grooved" to produce consistently good shots.

For a given distance, a pitch shot must be hit with more force (clubhead speed) than a chip shot. Some distance is taken off the pitch shot due to the higher ball flight. On the longer swing for the pitch shots (and the chip shots), the clubhead naturally swings inside the target line and then upward on the backswing and on the follow-through. Through the impact area, the clubhead travels on the target line and close to the ground. Some changes in addressing the ball accommodate the longer shots: A longer hold on the club handle produces more clubhead speed; a wider stance, square and balanced, allows a freer and fuller swing.

Situations Favoring the Chip Shot

If a high trajectory shot is not required and putting the ball from off the putting green has been ruled out, a chip shot (landing on or short of the putting green) is favored under any of the following conditions (fig. 5.10):

- The greens are dried out and hard: Pitch shots will not "hold" on the green.

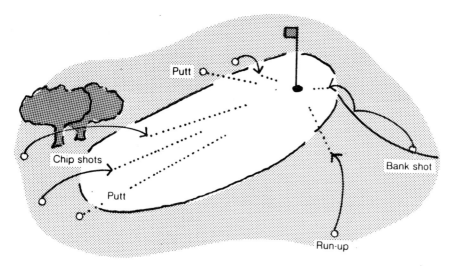

Figure 5.10
Approach situations.

- The ball is lying in a poor position, such as on sparse ground. Usually, it is less difficult to hit the ball from poor lies with medium-lofted irons.
- Play is in strong windy conditions. Low shots are less affected by the wind.
- A low shot is required as, for example, when hitting the ball under the limbs of a tree.
- An elevated area intervenes between the putting green and the ball and the space between the edge of the putting green and the hole is limited ("little green to work with"). Hit a low chip shot to strike the bank, rebound upward, and onto the putting green ("bump and run") shot.

Most golfers find it easier to judge how a ball will roll over the putting green after landing than to guess how a pitch shot will react upon hitting the putting green. Another consideration favoring the chip shot is that it usually requires a smaller swing (with less force) for a given distance. If an error, such as topping, is made, the error in shot result is likely to be less than it would be with the stronger hit pitch shot.

Situations Favoring the Pitch Shot

The pitch shot can be an effective stroke when the following conditions exist:

- The ball must be lofted into the air.
- The putting greens are relatively soft and will "hold" pitch shots.
- The ball lies in a good position on the turf.
- The space on the putting green is sufficient for the ball to land and come to rest close to the hole ("plenty of green to work with").

For longer approach shots played under these conditions, the pitch shot played to the putting green is preferred over the chip shot played to land short of the putting green. Sometimes, however, it is necessary to hit a pitch shot to land short of the putting green and then bounce forward onto the green ("pitch-and-run"). If the ball has to be lofted into the air and there is a sharp downhill roll to the hole (or if the cup is located close to the edge of the green), a pitch shot must be played to land on the apron—not on the putting surface. (In these situations, if a ball were played to the putting green, it would most likely roll well past the hole and possibly off the putting green.)

Today's players have become proficient in hitting pitch shots to the putting greens. The pitching wedge is favored for these shots, but good pitch shots can be made with the 9-iron or even the 8-iron. Trying to hit the ball an extra long distance with a wedge is a mistake. Hitting a pitch shot with a high-lofted iron may be a better shot than trying to "press" a wedge to the distance limit. Expert wedge shots take a good deal of practice and experience and ideal course conditions.

Practice Suggestions

- Picture the action of a playground swing—swinging back and forth, back and forth. Swing the clubhead in this rhythmic manner. Sweep the grass with each back-and-forth motion. Clubhead speed should be the same for the backswing and the forward swing. This continual motion creates certain details of form. The wrists "give" or bend, acting as hinges, allowing the clubhead to swing in a longer arc than the hands. The outward pull of the swing (centrifugal force) causes the left arm to swing in an extended position. The body and legs give in the direction of the swing. Without striking a ball, practice one swing at a time. Watch the clubhead sweep the grass at the start of the swing and through the impact area. Hold the finish of the swing and feel control of the club with the hands.

- Hit many chip shots from near the green. Practice until you are machine-like in performance. Pick out a spot on the green where the ball should land and visualize the desired shot. Aim to "sink" each shot. The shots failing to drop into the cup should stop very close to it.

- In changing from practicing chip shots to hitting pitch shots, you may sense a difference in the swings. For a given distance, hitting a pitch shot with a higher-lofted iron requires a longer swing. Wrist action is more responsive as the swing lengthens; thus, you may sense more wrist action in the pitch shot. The longer swing and the difference in clubhead weights and shaft lengths all contribute to what you feel about the stroke. This is a result. To deliberately try to develop two different swings is neither necessary nor recommended.

Ed Fiori, PGA Tour Member for 13 years.

- Work from short approaches to longer ones. Change the target both for distance and line of direction. Make mental notes on the different length shots, such as how much to "choke up" on the grip, the width of the stance, and the necessary length of swing.
- Practice stroking the ball from good lies on the turf. When you are hitting the shots well, try hitting the ball from both good and fair lies. Stroking the ball from other than a good lie is not so much a matter of learning how to do it, but rather a matter of facing the situation without anxiety. Avoid practice from poor lies if you are hitting unsatisfactory shots. Such practice tends to destroy confidence and disrupt a good swing pattern.
- Reverse the club and grip the shaft near the clubhead with the end of the handle about 6 inches from the ground. Swing the tip of the handle back and forth continually. Then take the regular grip on the handle and swing the clubhead. After the continual swinging, practice taking one swing at a time. You will definitely feel the clubhead after swinging the comparatively weightless handle. For even greater sensitivity to the clubhead and the touch of hand control, take the same swings with the eyes closed.
- Stand with your feet together and take an approximate half swing. This stance requires you to swing smoothly and in balance.
- Practice swinging in front of a mirror. Pay particular attention to the start of the swing and the clubhead arc.

Short strokes are an important part of your game. Spend the first part of every practice session on them.

For Review

1. Describe the probable action of the hands and wrists when a player attempts to hit ("scoop") the ball into the air. What is the usual path of the ball when this incorrect effort is made? How may the error be corrected?
2. In playing a long rather than a short approach shot, what changes should you make in addressing the ball? What effect do these changes have on the swing?
3. If you are playing a shot from off the putting green, what are your options regarding the flagstick? How would such conditions as the terrain and the distance from the hole affect your choice of an option?
4. Under what conditions would you choose to hit a chip shot to the putting green? A putt? A pitch shot?
5. Before playing a 7-iron shot, you decide that a ball flight lower than the normal trajectory is desirable. What changes would you make to accomplish this objective?

The Full Strokes—
Irons and Woods

6

Essentially, the swings taken to hit wood shots and iron shots are the same, although they may feel somewhat different. There are differences in shaft lengths, club balances, club weights, swing speeds, and swing arcs. In the wood swing, the clubhead path is closer and more level to the ground for a longer distance through the ball contact area than it is with the irons. The wood swing may feel more like a sweep than the swing with the irons. One often hears that, in playing an iron, there should be a feeling of hitting down on the ball. If exaggerated, this cue can lead to trouble. For some players, especially novices, the idea of hitting down on the ball may result in a poor swing and a poor shot. Whether you are hitting an iron or a wood shot, the primary objective is to *swing the clubhead to hit the ball out to a target.*

The Swing—A Look at the Full Swing and Some Analysis

Addressing the Ball

For a complete review, see Chapter 4. As shown in figure 6.1:

- A definite target is chosen within the player's distance potential.
- The stance is comfortable. The feet are approximately shoulder width apart.
- The arms hang easily from the shoulders. The left arm and the club shaft are in an approximate straight line.

Starting the Backswing

As shown in figure 6.2:

- The backswing is started slowly and smoothly with ease. No attempt is made to hurry, lift, or grab the club handle.
- The clubhead is swung back close to the ground. The hands, arms, and shoulders move as a unit, accompanied by a natural give of the legs and body.

Figure 6.1
Addressing the ball.

Figure 6.2
Starting the backswing.

- The feeling is one of swinging the clubhead straight back away from the ball, but after a certain point, the clubhead normally swings inside the intended line of ball flight. Halfway into the backswing, the hands, the easily extended arms, and the clubhead are approximately opposite the right side.

Top of the Swing

As shown in figures 6.3 and 6.4:

- The club shaft is approximately horizontal.
- The left arm is easily extended, maintaining the swing radius. The right elbow is bent and is pointing down and slightly away from the right side.
- The wrists are bent (cocked) and in a position approximately under the club handle.
- The shoulders and hips have turned. The left shoulder is about under the chin. To accommodate this body rotation, some weight has shifted to the right side, and the left leg and foot have responded in the direction of the swing. For most players, the left heel rises slightly from the ground.

Downswing

As shown in figures 6.5 and 6.6:

- No attempt is made to rush into the downswing; patience is important. When the start of the downswing "feels" slow, it is apt to be correct.

Figure 6.3
Top of the swing.

Figure 6.4
Top of the swing—side view.

Figure 6.5
Downswing.

Figure 6.6
Downswing—side view.

- The downswing is a blended gathering of forces for contacting the ball with a swiftly moving clubhead. These actions merge into one another.
  - The left heel returns to its original position on the ground, and the body weight begins to shift to the left side.
  - The hips shift slightly to the left, and the body starts to turn in the direction of the swing.
  - The arms swing downward, with the left arm remaining in its extended position and with the right elbow coming close to the side.
  - The wrists remain in a cocked position, reserving clubhead acceleration for a split second later.

Figure 6.7
Impact.

Impact

As shown in figure 6.7:

- The body is in a firm position of balance, contributing to the clubhead attaining optimum speed at ball contact.
- The clubhead catches up with the hands. The hands, arms, and clubhead move through the impact area together.
- The head remains fairly still.

Follow-Through

As shown in figures 6.8 and 6.9:

- Through the impact zone, the clubhead swings close to the ground and on the intended line of ball flight, and then gradually moves inside that line and upward.
- The objective—swinging the club to hit the ball to a distant target—along with the swiftly moving clubhead, produce a follow-through in good form.
  —The shoulders and hips turn so that the body is facing the intended target. Good balance is maintained.
  —The head turns and gradually rises to accommodate the full finish and to see the shot result.
  —The right knee bends and turns so that it is touching (or near) the left knee and pointing toward the target. The right heel is well off the ground.
  —The speed of the clubhead carries the arms up, continuing the circular motion of the swing, while the hands maintain their hold on the club.

Figure 6.8
Follow-through.

Figure 6.9
Finish of swing.

The Search for Distance—
Cautions and Suggestions

Progressing to the point of stroking the ball with the long irons and woods should not be a complicated step. The objective is to strike the ball to a more distant target, but a target within your distance potential. If the objective becomes hitting the ball with all your might, such complications as poor coordinations, muscle tensions, and poor timing arise. They are the curse of the beginner and experienced player alike.

Muscular Contraction and Relaxation

Some practical knowledge about muscle action is helpful. Try this experiment related to using muscles effectively and ineffectively. Extend your right arm out in front of you with your palm facing up. Bend the elbow and touch your fingers to your shoulder. Now again extend the arm, but this time tightly tense (contract) all the arm muscles. Keeping the muscles tense, try bending your elbow. This action is now difficult, if not impossible because you are preventing muscles used in the motion from performing. When you relax, they can perform easily. Tensing up when you want the arm to move is like stepping on a car's accelerator and brake at the same time.

When golfers try to hit the ball ''hard'' to get distance, they tend to use muscles that resist and even block the intended movement. Muscular contractions of resistance plus strong muscular contractions to overcome the resistance may make a swing feel powerful, but these contradictory efforts spell ruin for distance and accuracy. All players can be misled by the ''feeling'' of a golf swing. When a fine shot is hit a considerable distance, a player is apt to say: ''But I swung so easy.'' That is true. The muscle action was synchronized: Resistant actions were avoided, and the right contractions were made. The swing felt ''good.''

After hitting a beautiful long shot with an "easy" swing, you may theorize: "If I can hit that distance, why not 'put something into it' and get my full distance?" But what can you put into the swing? If it is more clubhead speed, then a longer shot can be expected. But if you are misled into "muscling the ball" (adding tension), then you will probably hit the ball a shorter distance. When the swing feels easy and possibly slow, you may be swinging with the best possible clubhead speed.

Timing the Swing

If you can avoid hurrying to hit the ball, your chances for developing and maintaining well-timed swings are good. Speeding up the swing to hit the ball great distances destroys tempo and rhythm and produces poor and painful golf shots. So much is put into the motion, and so little is gained. A well-timed swing produces accuracy and optimum speed at and through ball contact. Consider these suggestions to help time your swing:

- Since the swing is started from a motionless position, it must begin slowly and evenly. Then a gradual and smooth acceleration of the clubhead follows.
- The feet, legs, body, arms, and hands must work together, each supplying its own power. Arguing and trying to reach a decision on whether a particular body part plays a more important role in timing or in power is futile. The fact that you can move your hands and arms faster than you can move your body and legs furnishes a lead for timing. You cannot flail away with the hands and arms and have the legs and body trying to catch up by lunging and jerking. The arms and hands must be attuned to the speed at which the legs and body can move.
- Many players find that counting helps their swings. The backswing is counted as 1, the top of the swing 2, and the downswing 3; or 1—and—2; or back—and—through. Some players use only two counts; some use key words that have significance for them.
- Keep the same tempo and rhythm for all strokes. Key your timing to a medium iron and maintain the same tempo when you progress to the long irons and woods. Many players have ruined a golf game by keying their timing to fast swings with the driver. Players who rush to the golf course, take a few strenuous swings with the driver, and hit a few practice shots as hard as they can are likely to say: "My timing is off today."

The synchronization of a fine golf swing that produces accurate and long golf shots is beyond human description, but within human achievement.

Distances and Club Selection

The Irons

The distance range between the shortest and the longest iron is approximately 100 yards. Sometimes, however, players fail to hit the ball the expected distance with the longer irons. The probable reason, other than lack of practice or experience, is expending useless effort to hit the ball farther. Longer clubs should yield longer shots. Some players, tempted to hit the ball far, prevent the club from doing its job.

Through practice and experience, you learn just how far you can hit the ball with each iron. If the distance to the green calls for a 5-iron shot, hit the ball with that club. Avoid "pressing" a 6-iron. To score well, always use "enough club."

The amount of clubface loft of the irons ranges from about 20 to 50 degrees—hence, the different ball flight trajectories. For any specific iron, the flight trajectory may be changed by increasing or decreasing the clubface loft when addressing the ball. Increasing the loft ("opening the face") produces a higher than normal shot; decreasing the loft ("closing the face") produces a lower than normal shot.

The high-lofted irons are designed for a high degree of accuracy. A swing somewhat less than the full swing may be recommended for these clubs. This is sensible. Less movement is involved in a three-quarter swing than in a full swing; thus, there is a greater chance of being accurate. This motion is an extension of the half swing. No great effort need be made to increase the swing. With a purpose of stroking the ball a slightly longer distance, a longer swing naturally is taken. Some players use an approximate three-quarter swing for all the full iron shots and for the wood shots (fig. 6.10).

The Woods

The driver—the 1-wood—is designed to hit the ball from a tee. Only in unusual circumstances is it used from the fairway. Some players who find the driver a problem club, tee off with the 3-wood. Also, players may choose to drive with a fairway wood (or a long iron) when the hole is especially treacherous—as when hitting onto a very narrow fairway bordered by an out of bounds on one side and deep rough on the other side. Sacrificing some yardage for a chance of being accurate and avoiding trouble is good playing strategy.

In playing wood shots from the fairway, the ball's position on the ground is more important than any distance consideration in deciding what club should be used. The higher lofted woods are more effective in hitting from poor lies than is the 3-wood. For difficult and troublesome lies, even though the ball may be a wood distance from the hole, an iron shot may be the better choice.

Figure 6.10
Approximate three-quarter swing.

Practice Suggestions

- Take short and full swings without hitting a ball. To help increase left hand and arm strength, practice swinging while holding the club with only the left hand.
- To check for a steady head position on the backswing and downswing, stand so that your shadow casts in front of you and watch your head's shadow. Stay relaxed—avoid tightening the muscles of your upper body.
- Practice the exercises for developing the footwork and body turn (pivot) (figs. 6.11 and 6.12).
- Use common sense when practicing.
  - —Work from hitting short iron shots to the full shots. Warm up. Avoid beginning to practice by ''whaling away'' at the ball with the driver. Not only may muscle and joint strain occur, but such action can destroy a golf swing.
  - —Avoid extra long practice sessions. Break up the practice times with rest periods.
  - —When hitting iron shots from artificial turf or from hard ground, avoid trying to hit down on the ball or to take divots. The reverberation of the shock of hitting a hard surface could injure hands, wrists, arms, or shoulders.

Figure 6.11
Exercise 1 for developing footwork and body turn.

Figure 6.12
Exercise 2 for developing footwork and body turn.

- Swing (with or without a club) as though you were swinging a baseball bat. Start swinging to hit an imaginary ball at shoulder height, then waist height, then on the ground. Let the body and legs respond to the movement. Keep the swing smooth—do not try to hit home runs.
- If the long iron and the wood shots are unsatisfactory, try hitting shots with a shorter hold on the club. After some success, gradually work up to the full hold.
- If it is difficult to hit balls off the grass (irons and woods), tee up the balls. Then return to hitting balls from good lies. With confidence restored, you can stroke the ball from varying positions without anxiety.
- Practice hitting the ball to different specific targets. Change both line of direction and distance. Learn the specific distances you can hit the ball with each club.

Sam Snead, Courtesy of Wilson Sporting Goods Company.

Ricki Kawagishi, Member, Advisory Staff, Mizuno Golf Company.

Ayako Okamoto, Member, Advisory Staff, Mizuno Golf Company.

Keith Fergus, Member, Advisory Staff, Wilson Sporting Goods Company.

Beth Stone, Member, LPGA, Golf Stop Inc., Tuscon, Arizona.

Pat Bradley, Member of Team Mazda, Representative Yamaha Golf Company, LPGA Hall of Fame.

For Review

1. What does timing a swing mean to you? How can a well-timed swing improve your golf shots? What are some points to remember in developing a swing of proper tempo and rhythm?
2. You are failing to hit the ball farther with a 3-iron than with a 5-iron. What steps would you take to remedy this problem?
3. A steady head position is important in developing a consistent swing. How can you check on whether you maintain a steady head position as you swing?
4. Why is it important to swing with some ease rather than exert yourself to hit the ball hard? How can a feeling of "power" be misleading?

The Putting Stroke

7

If open putting tournaments were held—to include men and women, amateurs and professionals—betting only on the professionals to win would be unwise. Many average golfers are exceptionally skillful in putting. They have learned and developed an outstanding "touch and feel" for the stroke—something that cannot be taught. Accompanying this quality is a confidence, a sureness that they are good putters. This confident demeanor and the sense of touch and feel cannot be separated—they almost become one and the same. Without one, the other is impossible.

Quietly accepting the idea that you can be a good putter paves the way for your becoming one. Players who seem to revel in declaring themselves poor putters usually remain so—avoid joining them!

A confident attitude nourishes concentration. When the mind is free of doubt, it can focus on the job to be done—in this case, putting the ball into the hole. A gentle and quiet mental preparation, without self-harassment, can be the key to a successful putting game.

Addressing the Ball

Good putting requires a feeling of ease and a gentle seriousness. This attitude begins with a comfortable grip and stance.

The Hold on the Club

The reverse-overlapping grip is favored for putting by the majority of golfers (fig. 7.1). The hands are placed on the handle with the palms approximately facing each other and with the thumbs down the front of the shaft. The index finger of the left hand overlaps the little finger of the right hand, or extends downward and overlaps more than one finger. There is no one best grip. Players have become fine putters by holding the club in various styles, such as the ten-finger grip, a cross-handed grip (hands in reverse position on the handle), and the split-hand grip (hands a distance apart on the club handle).

Back view   Front view

Figure 7.1
Reverse-overlapping grip.

Figure 7.2
Putting stance (Michael Hemphill).

The Stance

Just as there is no best club and no best grip for putting, there is no best stance. Narrow to wide—square, open, closed—all are acceptable. The rules, however, prohibit standing with either foot touching or astride the line of putt. The line extends from the hole to a point beyond the ball (fig. 7.2).

Figure 7.3
Putting stroke.

Basic Points for Addressing the Ball

Even though there is some variation in grip and stance among good players, there is a general consensus on basics for addressing the ball:

- The club is held with a gentle firmness. The reverse-overlapping grip is favored.
- The club sole is flat on the ground with the clubface pointing to the target.
- The stance is taken close to the ball. The body is bent forward so that the eyes are directly above and looking straight down on the ball.
- The knees are bent and easy.
- The arms are relatively close to the body with the elbows bent. For steadiness, the right arm may rest against the right thigh.
- Similar to all golf shots, the ball is played from a point opposite the inside of the left heel to a point opposite the center of the stance. If the ball is played toward the left side, more weight may be carried on the left foot.

The Swing

The swing is a pendulum-like motion. The club is swung back and through close to the ground (fig. 7.3). For short distances, the clubhead is swung on the intended line of ball roll. On long putts, the feeling may be one of swinging the putterhead on the line, but as the swing increases in length, the clubhead may naturally swing slightly inside the intended line of putt on the backswing and follow-through. Being overly concerned about the exact clubhead path tends to "freeze" the swing and create tension. Also, thinking about the path is distracting, for attention is then diverted from the real purpose of the swing: *to roll the ball into the hole*. Rather than trying to "harness" the stroke, let the swing develop naturally.

Having a feeling for the correct line of play and swinging the putter close to the ground should create this simple swing. The subtle, combined movement of the hands, wrists, and arms blend into one swing. In this pendulum-like swing, the hands swing back and through with the clubhead. Avoid any detailed analysis of this swing; instead, work on developing a touch and feel for the stroke.

The body remains still. Its only contribution to the swing is to provide stability.

Aiming

To aim, simply draw an imaginary line of roll from the ball to the hole; then place the putter in back of the ball so that the clubface is perpendicular to this line. On a straight putt, the clubface will point to the line and the hole. On a sidehill putt, the clubface will point to a spot on the line, not to the hole. (On a sidehill putt, allowance must be made for the ball to roll down the sidehill.) The imaginary line of roll should be figured first from a position back of the ball, looking toward the cup. After the clubface is set so that it points to the target, the selected line of roll is confirmed. Some players find it helpful to place the clubhead in front of the ball to check the alignment of the clubface.

Make the procedure for addressing and stroking the ball simple. After setting the clubface so that it points to the target and taking a comfortable stance, sight down the intended line of roll, visualize the desired putt, and then run your eyes back along the line to the ball. Proceed to putt without delay.

Your goal should be to roll the ball into the hole. If the ball does not roll into the hole, have it come to rest inches away, for an easy second putt. The adage "never up, never in" makes sense. *Putt the ball as far as the hole: Only then does it have a chance to drop into the hole.*

Judgment Factors

In addition to estimating distances, you must judge how the ball will roll over the putting surface. "Reading" the green correctly is a must for good putting.

Putting greens are referred to as "fast" or "slow," depending on how easily the ball will roll over the surface. If the grass is sparse, dried out, or newly mowed, the putting green will be "fast." The opposite conditions will cause the putting green to be "slow." A bent type of grass influences the roll of the ball: A putt against the grain requires a firmer stroke than a putt rolling with the grain. Some allowance may have to be made when putting at an angle to the bent grass.

Figuring how the ball will roll over slopes and undulations (the "breaks" of the putting greens) is always interesting and often rewarding. To aim five feet to one side of the hole and then see your ball roll over your point of aim, gradually turn with the slope, and then drop into the hole is indeed a joy.

Standing behind your ball while waiting your turn to putt gives you a chance to study the line and to figure any breaks. From this vantage point, you can gather useful information by watching the roll of the putts made by other players.

Putting—The Key to Low Scores

The top tournament professional golfers—men and women—often shoot sub-par rounds. The key stroke in these rounds is the putt. If professional golfers were asked: "Of all the golf strokes, which one would you want at its peak during a tournament?" The answer would be unanimous: "Putting."

If par is 72 for a course, 36 strokes are allotted to reach the putting green and 36 strokes are assigned for putting. In a round of 18 holes, all players—from the novice to the professional—can expect to take fewer than 36 putts, but rarely can they expect to take fewer than 36 strokes to reach the putting greens. Reaching a putting green in the par figure allotted for a hole is commonly called either "being on in regulation" or "hitting the green."

Reading that a professional "hit 18 greens" or was "on in regulation" on all 18 holes tells you that the player was on the green in the distance allotment figures. What an opportunity for a fine score! On each hole, this golfer is putting for a score of one under par, a birdie. If the player scores six birdies and twelve pars, taking a total of 30 putts, the score for a par-72 course will be 66—a superb round of golf.

For a player to take 36 putts and score below par for a round would be very unusual because there are few greens, if any, that a player can reach in fewer than regulation figures. Par-5 holes for men and par-5 and par-6 holes for women can sometimes be reached in less than regulation by long hitters. If a player reaches the green of a par-5 hole in two shots or reaches the green of a par-6 hole in three shots, he or she is then putting for a score of 2 under par for the hole, an eagle. It is possible, but rare, for a player to reach the green of a par-4 hole in one stroke. The hole must be either especially short for its par or unusual conditions must exist, such as hard ground or wind aiding the distance of the shot from the tee.

Putting gives you chances to score under par on certain holes as well as to make up for any poor shots in your play from the tee to the putting green. *To score well, you must become a consistently good putter.*

Practice Suggestions

- Begin your practice with short putts. Line up several balls about a foot from the hole and simply stroke each ball into the cup with little or no thought on "how" to putt. Let your instinct for aiming and judging take over. Gradually increase the distance. Missed putts should come to rest very close to the hole.
- Stroke the ball and listen for it to drop into the hole. This will help train you to remain calm and confident, not anxious, about the result. The person who starts steering a putt immediately upon contacting the ball expects to miss the putt, not make it.
- Practice at home on carpeting. It does not matter if the surface is different from grass. You are practicing to develop a stroke and swing.
- When necessary, review some putting fundamentals. Then proceed to concentrate on sinking putts.
- After a session of starting with short putts and working back to long distances, try a variety of putts—short, long, uphill, downhill, sidehill, and from off the apron of the putting green. Practice lining up the putts without delay. Learn to size up the situation and to proceed at once to make the putt.
- If in practice or play the putts are "rimming" the hole, with many close putts and "just misses," do not fret. You are putting well. The putts will start dropping. Do not change this good stroke.
- On sidehill putts, visualize the curved path on which the ball must roll to drop into the hole. Pick out a spot on this path for your point of aim, as a bowler might do in spot bowling. Use such points as a different-colored section of grass or a dead blade of grass. (A dead blade of grass may be removed, but if it is an aid in aiming, make use of it. It will not deflect the roll of the ball.)
- Stroke the ball so that it will roll smoothly over the green. The ball should not bob up and down. It should hug the putting surface in a forward end-over-end roll—*overspin*. You can easily check the roll of the ball: Draw a circumference line around the ball with a colored marking pencil, place the ball in a position so that the marked line is in the vertical plane, and then stroke the ball and check to see whether the line stays in the same plane.
- To make your practice especially challenging, instead of putting for the hole, place a coin on the green and aim for it. After this practice, the hole may seem as large as a bushel basket, and your confidence in your putting may soar.
- For self-testing practice, play nine different holes of a practice putting course. Par would be eighteen for the nine holes. Check the number of strokes you are above or below par. Some of your practice may be in match or stroke competition with another player. This practice is enjoyable, stimulating, and challenging.

Jim Booros, Member, Advisory Staff, Acushnet Golf Equipment.

After you have gained some skill in putting, work on a smooth, easy, and comfortable stroke. Avoid a detailed analysis of the swing. Anyone who can swing a putter can learn to putt well. Good putting is up to you!

For Review

1. In judging how a putting green will affect the roll of the ball, what conditions should you note, and how should you adjust your stroke for each?
2. What is meant by the terms *being on in regulation* or *hitting the green?*
3. Review some basic points for addressing the ball in putting. What stance is prohibited by the rules?
4. What are some useful suggestions to follow in practicing putting? How much analysis of the swing should be made?

Special Consideration Shots

8

Shooting from a bunker, striking the ball from hillside lies, hitting the ball from the rough, or playing shots in windy conditions requires some adjustments and changes. A positive attitude and sound practice in applying some basic techniques will yield satisfactory and good shots.

Playing from a Bunker (Sand)

To make golf more interesting and challenging, bunkers are placed strategically on the course. The rule book refers to these areas by the proper name, *bunkers;* some people, however, call them sand traps. In bunkers, creeks, and lakes (all defined as hazards), the surface of the area may *not* be touched before taking the forward swing to strike the ball. The club may *not* be grounded in the address position as in other shots (fig. 8.1). (It is permissible to take a practice swing, provided the surface of the hazard is not touched.)

Bunkers vary from course to course. Some are shallow, with a thin layer of sand spread over a hard surface; others are deep pits with almost vertical walls and with soft, powdery sand several inches deep. (A ball landing in some bunkers may bury itself.) The vision of standing in a pit with almost vertical walls and with the golf ball partially buried in the sand is dismal. Yet, players of varying skills are able to hit outstanding shots in such circumstances.

From a shallow bunker with no overhanging turf ("lip") and with the ball lying in a good position on the sand, few, if any, adjustments need to be made. From a fairway bunker, use a club in which you have confidence. Aim to hit the ball before touching the sand with the clubhead. If the shallow bunker is adjacent to the green, consider playing a stroke similar to a chip shot. Or, if after checking the area between the bunker and the putting green, you believe a ball can roll easily out of the sand and over the grass, then use the putter and putt the ball onto the green.

When the ball lies in a deep bunker bordered by overhanging turf, or when the ball is in a poor lie (partially buried in a footprint), an "explosion" shot must be played (fig. 8.2). For this shot, use a sand wedge or the highest-lofted club in your set. Open the clubface when addressing the ball. Most players prefer taking an open stance. Whatever stance is taken, make it comfortable and plant your feet into the sand. Play the ball opposite the left side of the stance. Depending on the sand texture and the desired distance, aim to strike the sand one to three inches back of the ball. Look at that selected spot, not at the

Figure 8.1
Addressing the ball—sand shot (Michael
Hemphill).

Figure 8.2
"Explosion" shot from bunker (Michael Hemphill).

ball. The clubhead sweeps through the sand and under the ball. Both the ball and the "cushion" of sand between the clubface and ball are propelled forward at impact. Complete the swing by swinging through the sand and the ball.

Other useful tips for sand play follow:

- The primary objective for all bunker shots is to hit the ball out of the sand in the initial stroke. Avoid having to play another shot from the bunker.
- Be willing to modify distance objectives when playing from fairway bunkers. Use a club in which you have confidence and one with enough loft to hit the ball out of the sand.
- To establish a stable stance, wiggle your feet into the sand. A stance slightly wider than normal may also provide stability.
- The rules prohibit testing the surface of the bunker. However, you cannot help but gather useful information about the condition of the sand and surface when you walk into the bunker and when you take your stance.
- A shorter, more controlled swing may serve best in hitting distance shots from fairway bunkers. Such a swing may provide more accuracy so that the ball can be hit cleanly from the sand. Limit body motion (pivot) during sand shots because the stance in sand is less stable.
- Always remember to swing the clubhead through the ball (or sand). Never try to scoop the ball. The hands must maintain a strong position through impact, especially in the explosion shot.

Playing from Hillside Lies

In playing from hillside lies, follow the adage: "Don't make a mountain out of a molehill." In stroking the ball from a slight, gentle slope, play the shot almost as you would any comparable shot on level ground. Trust your instinctive sense of feel to guide you in taking a comfortable, balanced stance. When playing from steeper slopes, you may need to make certain adjustments. Take a practice swing on the slope to get a feel for a balanced stance and for the automatic swing adjustments that will occur due to the different posture necessary in addressing the ball. Whatever your situation, keep your plans simple.

When playing from uphill or downhill lies, play the ball opposite an area favoring the higher side of the stance. Make an allowance in aiming to counteract the tendency to hit the ball off line: When hitting uphill, aim slightly to the right; downhill, slightly to the left (figs. 8.3, 8.4). To avoid accidentally moving the ball when addressing it, either place the clubhead a few inches back of the ball or hold it slightly above the ground.

On sidehill lies with the ball above the feet, taking a shorter hold on the club may be helpful, depending on the amount of slope. Keep your weight forward toward the toes to avoid falling back away from the ball on the swing. Aim slightly right to compensate for the tendency to hit left.

Figure 8.3
Uphill lie.

Figure 8.4
Downhill lie.

On a sidehill lie with the ball below the feet, settle your weight back toward the heels to avoid losing your balance forward and aim slightly to the left.

Playing from the Rough

Conditions in the rough vary. Sometimes, there is little difference between the rough and the fairway except that the turf off the fairway may be sparse. But when the grasses and undergrowth are long and heavy, and the ball nestles down into the area, problems arise. In such situations, the only objective is to hit the ball out of the rough and onto a clear area.

To send the ball quickly into the air and above the rough, use a high-lofted club, and if necessary, open the clubface. To avoid interference from the long or heavy growth back of the ball, swing the clubhead more upright on the backswing. (This is sometimes referred to as a V-swing, as opposed to the more usual U-shaped swing.)

Maintain a firm, not tense, hold on the club throughout the stroke. Swing the clubhead through the ball and grass. In addressing the ball or in removing loose impediments, be careful that you do not accidentally move the ball and incur a one-stroke penalty.

Playing in the Wind

Playing golf in a strong wind is generally more difficult than playing on a calm day. "Don't fight the wind" is probably the best advice for play on windy days. Avoid tensing up and trying to do the impossible. Adapt your game to the conditions that exist, but do not completely abandon good scoring objectives.

Taking a shorter swing for distance shots may prove helpful. Better balance can be maintained with the possibility of a more effective swing and more accurate shot results. Avoid speeding up your swing tempo to get distance.

When the wind is blowing in the same direction as your intended long-distance shots, take advantage of the situation. Hit higher shots, letting the wind carry the ball farther. When the wind is blowing against you, hit low-trajectory shots. If feasible, use a longer club for more distance; otherwise, be satisfied with less than normal distance. If the wind is blowing across the line of play, aim your shot into the wind to allow for the carry of the ball in the wind direction.

To check the wind direction, note how the pennant on the flagstick is blowing, or toss some blades of grass into the air and note the wind's direction and force.

For Review

1. What is the most important objective in making a bunker shot? What are the recommended procedures if you find your ball in the following situations: partially buried in a bunker adjacent to the putting green, lying well up on the sand in a shallow bunker adjacent to the putting green, lying in a heel print 180 yards from the hole?
2. On a very windy day, how should you adjust your shots according to the following wind directions: blowing against you, blowing in the direction of your target, blowing across the line of play?
3. Why is it advisable to shift the body weight in the stance preparatory to playing a ball on a sidehill lie? In which direction should the shift be when the ball lies below the feet? Above the feet?
4. How does a V-swing differ from a U-swing? In what situations would you choose to use the V-swing?

Improving Your Golf Game

9

When it comes to improving your golf game, you are the coach, teacher, psychologist, and confidant or confidante. The information you gather from lessons and other sources will help in laying out a program for hitting better shots and shooting lower scores. But your success really depends on you.

Attitude and Concentration

- Confidence, the necessary ingredient for playing good golf, cannot be fantasy; it must be something real, based on the experience of striking many successful golf shots. You, like thousands of other golfers, can develop and improve your skill in the game through practice and playing.
- Applying negative labels to yourself, such as "I can't putt," "I can't aim," and "I can't use my 3-wood," leads to poor play. (Also, such statements spoken aloud are both boring and distracting to playing companions.)
- Accept responsibility for your shots. What someone else says or does should not affect your game adversely. Blaming anyone or any "bad break" for a poor shot makes little sense. Keep control of your game; then you can improve it.
- Golf requires patience and perseverance. Do not be disheartened by one or a few poor shots. An errant or "dubbed" shot may be a blessing in disguise: A fine recovery stroke may stimulate you to play an excellent round. Avoid letting yourself get "down." Perhaps, some brilliant shots still lie ahead.
- Golf requires concentration, exclusive attention to the shot being played, with no extraneous and disquieting thoughts. An often-heard expression about a poor shot is, "I didn't take enough time to concentrate." The implication that taking more time will assure concentration is erroneous. Time may allow disturbing and fearful ideas to enter into the planning. Be orderly and concise, select your objective, visualize the shot, and proceed to play the ball.
- "Playing" an opponent can take your mind off your game. Let your worthy opponent be you. Figure your best possible score for each hole and then compete against it (fig. 9.1).

Charting your golf games can be enjoyable and interesting—and may help lower your scores.

Set a **target score** for each hole: the best, reasonable score you can make on the hole. Each time that pre-set score is made, circle it on the score card. At the end of the round, total your 18-hole score and count the number of target scores.

Plot both scores on a chart similar to the one shown here. (The ranges you select for the 18-hole scores and the target scores may differ from those in the sample.) This player figured the range of target scores from 4 up to 14, and the 18-hole scores from 86 down to 76. (Note that space was provided for even better scores.) The date, course, and course rating are recorded at the top of each score line.

Keeping these records may improve your game because:

- Even if you score poorly on a hole early in a round, you keep your enthusiasm and poise for playing well on the remaining holes. You maintain your goal—to shoot a target score on each hole.
- Instead of "playing" an opponent, you compete against your best scores, which is the ideal competition.

Figure 9.1
Charting your way to better golf.

- Being too intent may take the joy out of golf and slow down your progress. Remember that a certain amount of relaxation is necessary to swing the club effectively. Golf is a game for pleasure. Enjoy it.

Lessons

As long as you play golf, you will take golf lessons—either from a golf teacher or from yourself in the form of self-coaching. This is the experience of all golfers, even the expert tournament professionals.

To profit most from lessons:

- Be physically ready to take a lesson. Do warm-up exercises and practice hitting some golf balls. Without this preparation, part of your lesson will be warm-up time, instead of all lesson time.
- Work with your instructor. When you are taking lessons, avoid working on pet theories of your own. To do an effective job of teaching, your instructor must know what you are trying to do.
- When you are given a cue about your swing, do not expect a miracle with the next shot. The result of a shot or two is not absolute proof of the worth or worthlessness of instruction.
- When you try to change a swing per instruction, the change may feel drastic; yet, little or no change may be visible to a teacher. At such times, trust the instructor's observation.
- Golf classes provide general instruction in the fundamentals and some individual coaching. There is good reason for individual help because all swings do not develop the same. The coaching given one person may not be useful to another.
- Avoid feeling disappointed and that you are failing to receive your money's worth if your instructor implies or says that your swing looks fine and that what you need is practice and play, not more instruction in swing analysis.

Self-Coaching

Intelligent self-coaching builds your golf game; poor self-coaching destroys it. Your future golf game may be influenced most by your own teaching.

- If you have a persistent problem, taking a lesson from a competent teacher instead of continuing to work alone may save much frustration and time.
- You can gather a mass of data on golf swings from reading, taking lessons, watching expert golfers, and listening to other players. Be intelligent and discriminating in evaluating these ideas. Are the concepts sound, and do they apply to you? Accumulating information has a bad and a good side: You may ''jam'' your brain with too much data, or you may be enlightened by a new and different approach to the swing.

- When poor shots pop into your game, do not panic and instantly begin a corrective program. Hitting a golf ball well requires precision. Anyone can have a lapse. If your stroke has been fairly consistent, give it a chance to return; do not tear it apart. If one club is giving you trouble, put it away and forget it. Later, practice with the club for short periods. Think about what to do right—not "What did I do wrong?"
- Remember—the hands are the connecting link with the club. They direct and transmit power. A fine sense of control with the fingers and hands is necessary to stroke the ball well. Sense the hands directing and controlling clubhead action.
- Theories abound for hitting golf shots and correcting swings. At practice ranges, you can get "free" lessons by asking almost any player for advice. The value of some pointers is questionable, however. While many golfers like to relate the secrets to their success, their advice often varies from day to day: A tip that seems a miraculous cure one day is discarded the next.

Fitness for Golf—Some Thoughts

Many athletes participate in training programs to increase their skills and to avoid joint and muscle strain. Well-chosen exercises can help to attain these goals as well as contribute to everyday good health. But what exercises should be chosen? Books, articles, audio and video cassettes, and television programs overwhelm us with calisthenic choices.

Serious thought was given to presenting a series of conditioning exercises for golfers in this text. But an exercise program should begin, not with exercise, but with the individual—a consideration of the person's needs, present capabilities, and physical habits—which makes including one series of exercises for all readers questionable. In addition, in the short space that can be allotted to this subject in a golf book, the ramifications of exercise—such as precautions, uses, and exact details of performance—cannot be adequately explored. The content of this book, therefore, has been confined to *golf* and to suggestions about how to make the best use of the physical activity of the game.

Perhaps the simplest and best advice for golfers is this: If you now walk the course, *keep walking*. If at present you are not walking the course but are physically able to do so, *start walking*. Leg strength is essential in swinging a golf club effectively. Keep your leg muscles in good tone, and treat your body and feet to the pleasure of treading on soft, grassy turf for about three miles.

Players required by the course management to rent and use a motorized cart should arrange with their riding partners to alternately walk and ride every other hole. Those players choosing to use a motorized cart because carrying a full, heavy set of clubs is too much of a burden can try carrying a partial set in a lightweight bag. The benefits derived from walking may be a good trade for using fewer clubs. Besides, some players discover little, if any, change in their games if they use fewer clubs.

One prominent golfer refers to the game played by golfers able to walk the course, but who choose to ride in a motor vehicle, as "cart golf." It is easy to agree with this golf purist: Too many people are failing to play the traditional game of golf, and too many are failing to derive its potential physical benefits.

Another piece of advice is to know what your body is capable of doing and accept its limitations. Use your body effectively; do not abuse it. Avoid attempting to swing a club in a fashion unsuitable to you.

The old cliché, "Keep your head down," leads overzealous followers of advice into trouble. On a full swing, they attempt to keep their heads in the address position long after the ball has been struck. Besides destroying the swing through the ball, this attempted restriction can lead to a real pain in the neck!

A questionable swing cue for some players is to keep the left heel flat on the ground in the backswing of a full swing. Golfers with great flexibility may have no difficulty with this restriction. But for the less supple golfer, trying to coil the upper body while inhibiting the turn and natural "give" of the lower body and legs is useless and risky. A free swing is difficult. Strenuously working one part of the back against a resisting part may cause a healthy back to become sensitive and a sensitive one to become painful. (Most golfers allow the left heel to rise slightly from the ground in the backswing of a full swing.)

Nothing is so tempting to golfers as the idea of lengthening their drives. One cue for this universal wish is to shift your hips forward on the downswing to get your body into the shot. Recalling the verse of a song may serve as a warning against taking this cue too seriously: "The thigh bone's connected to the hip bone, the hip bone's connected to the backbone, the backbone's . . ." With a "super-distance" vision in mind, some golfers violently thrust their hips forward. But an exaggerated hip movement that does not blend in with the whole swing is useless and may render a person unfit for golf (suffering from a sacroiliac sprain and painful distress signals).

Golf swings vary because people vary. Fortunately, we can all develop good form that suits our particular body build and condition. When golfers attempt to move or restrict movement in ways that tax the body's natural ability, nothing is gained, and a good deal may be lost.

Three Errors in Ball Contact

Topping

A topped ball is hit above its center, thus imparting topspin to the ball (fig. 9.2). The ball may travel in the air a short distance and then dive to the ground, or it may just roll along the ground.

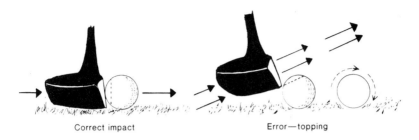

Correct impact   Error—topping

Figure 9.2
Topping the ball.

Attempting to hit the ball up into the air or to get under the ball often results in a topped shot. With such incorrect ideas in mind, the player is apt to swing the clubhead sharply upward through the impact zone, thus contacting the ball above its center. The strong, upward clubhead action causes the head and body to move up. The body weight may fail to shift properly to the left foot; in extreme cases, the weight may shift back to the right side, with the left heel coming off the ground.

Another common error causing a topped shot is changing the focus of attention from the execution of the stroke to its result. Instead of completing a good swing through the ball, the tense and anxious player looks up quickly to see, "What happened!?"

The early upward motion of the head at ball contact has fostered the most widely used correction of golf swings: "Keep your head down." The problem with using only this cue is that the real error is not addressed. The ball is topped with the clubhead—not the cranium. To correct the error of topping, attention should center on the cause of the error—incorrect clubface and ball contact—not on one symptom.

The following cues can be helpful in eliminating the error of topping:

• Select the correct purpose for the swing: to contact the ball squarely and hit it to the target. The clubface loft, not any swing effort, will loft the ball into the air.

• Focus on the complete swing. Be patient about seeing the shot result.

• Avoid flinching through the impact area. The act of drawing away from the ball with the shoulders and arms pulls the clubhead up. Keep the shoulders and arms easy.

• Swing the clubhead low through the impact area. If the ball is hit from a tee, sweep out the tee as the ball is struck; if from the grass, sweep the grass after striking the ball.

• In addressing the ball, instead of looking at the top of the ball, watch a spot at the back of the ball where contact should be made.

• Think: "Hit the ball so it will travel low." With this thought in mind, the clubhead is likely to be swung close to the ground through impact.

Result of incorrect
impact—shank

Practice tip—swing
to avoid striking the tee

Figure 9.3
The shank shot.

Striking the Ground Before Ball Contact—"Fat" Shot

A "fat" shot occurs when, instead of swinging the hands, along with the clubhead, through the impact area, the player attempts to "flip" the clubhead at the ball. The clubhead is sent forward, while the hands and wrists almost come to a stop. To correct the error, attention must be directed to maintaining the forward swing of the hands and the club. When the correction is made, the player may feel that the hands and wrists are leading the clubhead through impact (see fig. 5.5). Once a player hits several "fat" shots, especially in attempting to hit pitch shots over a bunker, a feeling of apprehension arises when another such shot must be played.

Shanking the Ball

If shanking the ball were a common fault, the population of golfers might decrease considerably. Shanking may be the most exasperating error in golf. This shot is hit with an iron, and the ball is contacted near the neck of the club, the rounded surface at the heel of the clubface. When the ball is struck with this rounded surface, the ball "squirts" out to the right. The player experiences a feeling of total ineffectiveness. Some fortunate golfers have never or rarely shanked a shot. Those unfortunate players who go through periods of shanking might do better seeing a psychiatrist than a golf teacher. The word *shank* is taboo in golf conversation—golfers fear that the mere mention of the word will bring on the error! Opinions on corrections would fill a book, but the following are possible solutions:

- Go back to the simple. Practice hitting short approach shots with a medium iron and work up to longer iron shots. Unless the swing is completely off, this may be the best correction, since it involves working on the positive and not fighting a fault.
- Avoid picking up the club on the backswing and applying extra effort either at the start of the downswing or near ball impact. These actions can force the clubhead forward and outside of the intended ball flight line.
- Placing a tee in the ground just beyond the toe of the clubhead and then swinging to avoid hitting the tee can help to correct the clubhead path (fig. 9.3).

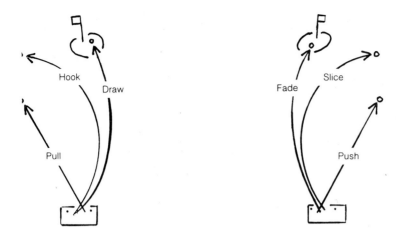

Figure 9.4
Directional paths of golf shots (right-handed players).

- Check the spot on the clubface where the ball is addressed. Addressing the ball out toward the toe of the clubface to allow for any error may be of temporary help.

Directional Flight Errors

Why a golf shot travels off line to the right or left of the intended target should not be a mystery. To demonstrate how you can stroke a ball off line, try this experiment using a putter: Putt a ball to a target about five feet away. Then, keeping the same stance and grip, putt a ball to the right of the target. Now stroke a ball to the left of the target. If the ball rolled straight to the right or left, the putter face was at right angles to the clubhead path. If the ball rolled in a curved path with clockwise or counterclockwise spin, then the clubface was not perpendicular to the path of the club.

In baseball or softball, players hit balls to left, center, and right fields by timing the swings so that the bat faces the target at impact. No change of stance is necessary. In tennis or table tennis, players hit shots to right, center, or left courts; they even purposely put spin on the ball to deceive their opponents.

Whether the sports implement to strike a ball is a golf club, bat, or racket, the position of the striking surface and its path at ball contact determine the flight of the ball. This basic information is useful when examining errors in the directional flight of the golf ball.

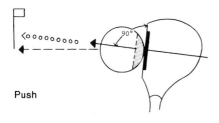

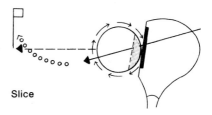

Push

Slice

Push—Straight shot to right of target
- Clubhead path through impact is on a line toward the right of the target—from inside-out.
- Clubface is perpendicular to the clubhead path.

Slice—Ball curves to right due to clockwise (horizontal) spin
- Clubhead path through impact can be: (1) on a line to the target, (2) from outside-in, (3) from inside-out.
- Clubface is pointing to the right of the clubhead path.

Figure 9.5
Push and slice.

Push and Slice

Both push and slice shots travel to the right of the intended target. In a *push* shot, the path of the clubhead through the contact area is on a line toward the right of the target, and the clubface is perpendicular to this line. This produces a straight shot but off line to the right.

In a *slice,* the path of the clubhead through contact can vary, but the clubface in relation to the path is open or facing to the right. This contact produces a horizontal, clockwise spin on the ball. As the spinning ball travels through the air, it curves to the right (fig. 9.5).

In considering the following corrections for these errors, assume that the grip and stance are correct and that the swing appears to be in good form:

- Being a fraction late in swinging the clubface to the square position at ball contact results in errant shots to the right. The ever-present urge to add effort at impact may cause the player to push the handle, leaving the clubface open. Also, a "quitting action" caused by anxiety and fear prevents the clubface from reaching the square position. Instead of confidently swinging the clubhead and maintaining the correct swing posture through impact, the player rises up, "comes off the ball," and leaves the clubface pointing to the right. Directing attention to swinging the clubface to the square position should help to correct these errors.
- If leaving the clubface open at impact has been a persistent problem, it may feel as if the clubface is closed when it is finally swung to the square position. (But the proof here is not in the feel but in the flight of the ball.) In some cases where the wrong feeling has been established, it is necessary to exaggerate—to try to swing the clubface to the closed position at ball contact. If, after such an attempt, the ball travels straight

to the target, the face was square at impact, no matter what the player felt. If the ball traveled to the left, an overcorrection was made.

- When the ball first travels to the left and then curves to the right of the intended target, the clubhead path is from "outside-in." This action may be the result of trying to avoid a slice, trying to steer the ball away from the right. The cure may be taking many practice swings in the correct path. Visualize the correct path through impact and swing on that line. Cut a swath of grass with the clubhead to check the path.
- Avoid trying to steer the ball straight or to get a straight follow-through. Trust that the swiftly swinging clubhead will travel in the correct path and strike the ball squarely.
- A poor correction is aiming to the left of the target. Such a practice fails to correct the error and usually compounds it.

An often-heard correction for slicing is "hit from inside-out." This may have some value for the person who has a very distorted swing, with the clubhead traveling from far outside and across the intended line of flight. Following only the cue "swing from inside-out," however, may increase the error of hitting to the right. The path of the clubhead through the contact area should be from inside the intended line—on the intended line—and then inside again (see fig. 3.3).

A closed stance is suggested frequently to correct slicing. If the player takes a closed stance and has a feeling of aiming to the right, and then compensates for this aim by swinging the clubface over to direct the ball to the intended target, this stance would be an aid. But changing the stance does not necessarily change the direction of the shot. Trick-shot artists prove this: They can take any stance, stand on one foot, or even sit down and hit the ball in any direction they choose. The path of the clubhead through the impact area and the relation of the clubface to this path determines the directional flight of the ball.

Pull and Hook

Both pull and hook shots travel to the left of the intended target. In the *pull* shot, the path of the clubhead through the contact area is on a line toward the left of the target, and the clubface is perpendicular to this line. This produces a straight shot but off line to the left.

In a *hook* shot, the path of the clubhead can vary, but the clubface in relation to the clubhead path is closed or facing to the left. This contact produces a horizontal, counterclockwise spin of the ball. As the spinning ball travels through the air, it curves to the left (fig. 9.6). The errors of pulling and hooking are less common than pushing and slicing. Consider the following points to correct for the pull or hook:

- Check the grip, especially the right hand. If the club is held with the right palm facing skyward, an errant shot to the left is likely. During the swing, the right hand is apt to return to a more natural position, thus closing the clubface.

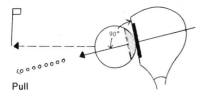

Pull

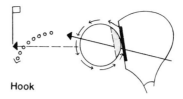

Hook

Pull—Straight shot to left of target
- Clubhead path through impact is on a line toward the left of the target—from outside-in.
- Clubface is perpendicular to the clubhead path.

Hook—Ball curves to left due to counterclockwise (horizontal) spin
- Clubhead path through impact can be: (1) on a line to the target, (2) from inside-out, (3) from outside-in.
- Clubface is pointing to the left of the clubhead path.

Figure 9.6
Pull and hook.

- To change a habit of swinging the clubhead to a closed position at impact, it may be necessary to try to swing the clubhead through the ball with a feeling that the clubface is open. If the ball travels straight after such an effort, the clubface was square at ball contact.
- Trying to hit the ball an extra long distance and "slapping" at the ball often result in hooking the ball. The right hand overpowers the left in the impact zone, thus closing the clubface. When this error is corrected, the player may sense a dramatic change in the swing. It may feel as though the left hand and arm are in control of the downswing and follow-through and that the right hand is doing little or nothing to strike the ball.
- If you consistently pull the ball to the left of the target, check your stance and the ball position in relation to your feet. When a player pulls a ball, it may be obvious that he or she has turned the body too early in the impact zone. Fear of hitting to the right may cause a player to turn on the ball to direct it away from such a directional error.

At times, skilled players intentionally stroke a ball so that it curves in flight and ends up on target. The *draw* shot curves in flight from right to left, the *fade* shot from left to right. Changing the grip may affect the alignment of the clubface, thereby altering the directional ball flight (figs. 4.8, 9.4).

Playing Hints

- Be ready to play golf. Warm up before you play. Before stepping on the first tee, practice swinging the club, starting with the short swing. Do gentle stretching exercises and hold the stretch a few seconds. Avoid violent or "bouncing" exercises. Make easy movements that will relax the shoulder and neck area. As you play your round, stay easy so that you can use your muscles efficiently.

- Learn the golf rules. Ignorance of the rules may cost you penalty strokes. Privileges extended by the rules may prove advantageous; for instance, when you drop a ball back of a water hazard, you may choose a well-kept area of grass on which to drop the ball, provided that all the other provisions of the rules are followed.
- Play according to the rules and keep your score accurately. To do otherwise is deceiving yourself.
- Golf should be a congenial and friendly game. When all players are considerate of each other, the game is enjoyable. The golf course is not the place for a lot of talk and idle chatter.
- If the course is in poor condition, improving the lie of the ball on the fairway (preferred lies or winter rules) may be condoned. Continued play of winter rules, however, is not golf. Accept the game's challenge—play the ball as it lies.
- Do not complain about the course. You choose the course; it does not choose you.
- No instruction on how to swing a club should be given during a round. Swing cues given during play are seldom appreciated; usually, they are distracting to both coach and student.
- Assume that you are teeing off at a hole with an out of bounds along the right side of the fairway. Tee the ball toward the right side of the teeing ground and aim to shoot to the center or slightly left of center of the fairway. In similar circumstances, use this strategy of aiming away from trouble.
- In playing approach shots or putts from off the putting green, the flagstick may be attended, removed from the hole, or left in the hole. If the ball is played from off the putting green, there is no penalty if it strikes the unattended flagstick. When playing a shot from off the putting green, most players prefer to have the flagstick left in the hole and unattended. Sometimes, the stick acts as a backstop for a firmly hit or downhill shot. The ball may fall into the hole or end up inches away from the cup if and when it strikes the flagstick.
- Tee up the ball when playing an iron shot from the tee. It is easier to hit a ball from a tee than from the ground. To avoid possible interference by the tee when hitting with a high-lofted iron (the tee and the ball could be contacted simultaneously), loosen the turf (especially hard ground) around the tee as you place it in the turf, or use a broken tee. If the tee is struck, it can fly out of the ground easily, offering no resistance (fig. 9.7).
- Think of and play one shot at a time. Have a clear purpose for each stroke. Avoid building up concern and tension about the next shot. For example, you see the ball roll into a distant bunker. The shot cannot be played from a distance—relax. When you reach the bunker, size up the situation, plan the shot, and play it.
- To select the correct club for a shot, consider: (1) the lie of the ball, (2) the desired distance, (3) special requirements for the situation, (4) course conditions, and (5) your skill with the different clubs. If the choice is

Possible interference
from tee

Use of broken tee
to avoid interference

Figure 9.7
Hitting an iron shot from tee.

    between two clubs in which you have equal confidence, generally play
the longer club to the green. Being short of the green ("underclubbing")
is a common fault.

- Learn different distances to the greens by spotting various objects, such
  as trees, bushes, and bunkers. Learn the "breaks" of the greens. Plan the
  most advantageous way to play each hole. Adjust your game to the course.

- If the ball is lying in a difficult position, on sparse grass, or on bare
  ground, take a practice swing over a spot similar in nature (if such a spot
  is near your ball). You have then faced the situation and will be less apt
  to be concerned about the lie.

- Play a safe shot if a daring one might put you in great trouble. If playing
  a safe shot costs an extra stroke to reach the putting green, a one-putt
  green may make up for the stroke.

- Play your own game of golf. If your distance limit for a 7-iron is 120
  yards, do not be challenged to hit 140 yards with a 7-iron simply because
  a member of your group can do so. Your objective is to score well, not to
  compete in a distance contest.

- Keep a record of your putts. In a corner of the scoring square for each
  hole, place a number indicating putts for the hole.

- Study your game after playing. If the game was fair or poor, what caused
  the trouble? Your swing? Carelessness? Lack of concentration? No
  warm-up? Too many putts? What are the solutions? If, however, you
  played a good or superb game, relax and enjoy the great feeling. You may
  even sit back and contemplate: "If a couple more of those putts had
  dropped. . . ."

Instructions for the New Player

Your first experiences in playing golf can be especially pleasant if you are prepared to go on the course—that is, if you have acquired some skill in the strokes and have a good general knowledge of the game.

- You should be able to answer "yes" to the following questions:
  —Are you able to sink many putts of two to three feet in length?
  —On longer putts of 25 feet or more, can you hole out in two strokes 50 percent of the time?
  —Have you developed some consistency in hitting shorter approach shots? Do you know which clubs to use for chip and pitch shots? Do you know how much to choke up on the club and how much swing to take for various distances, such as 20, 40, and 60 yards?
  —Have you developed some consistency in hitting the ball with the full swing? Do you know approximately how far you can hit the ball with each of the clubs in your set?
  —Have you carefully studied and learned the safety precautions, the etiquette, and the golf rules? Are you willing to watch the conduct of the experienced golfer and to learn from your observations?
- The following suggestions will help you:
  —If available, play a course consisting of short holes. If your only choice is a full-length course, plan your game when the course is not crowded.
  —In early games, most, if not all, players experience some anxious and tense times. To lessen and relieve these moments, playing every other hole allows time to relax, and just as important, time to learn by observing the play of others.
  —If possible, have an experienced golfer guide you in correct conduct. But remember, no lengthy or detailed instruction should be asked for or given while playing on the course.
  —You will most likely take more strokes than other players. You can help make up the time by walking rapidly between shots and by being alert to play in your group. Avoid delaying play.
  —If necessary, be willing to modify your game to avoid delaying the play of others. For example, you have made several attempts to hit the ball from deep rough without success. Either pick up your ball and toss it in the fairway, or discontinue play on the hole and resume play at the next tee. You will be relieved of concern and tension; your playing companions and other golfers on the course will appreciate your thoughtfulness. Scores for early games are not so important that they merit delaying play.
  —Golf is a complicated game. Be patient. With practice, study, and experience, you will soon be playing golf as it should be played.

For Review

1. What determines the flight direction of the golf ball?
2. How does the ball flight differ in the slice and push shots? Describe how the clubface must contact the ball to produce these shots. What are some possible corrections for these errors?
3. Why may trying to hit the ball up into the air cause the very error it is intended to correct? What are some possible corrections for the error of topping the ball?
4. Slow play continues to be a problem on the golf course. How can you, no matter what your skill, help to alleviate this problem?
5. What steps can you take to improve your game and enjoy it more?

Essential Knowledge

10

No matter what your golfing skill, you can be well-informed in golf knowledge and procedures. You can make yourself a welcome member of any golfing group by knowing and observing the accepted traditional conventions of the game.

Etiquette

The rules of etiquette are not strict formalities that complicate play; rather, they simplify and enhance the game. Observance of these rules makes it possible to play better golf and to enjoy the game more, to keep the course in good condition, and to allow more people to play golf by speeding up play. Strict adherence to the rules of etiquette should be routine practice for all players.

Creating a Quiet Atmosphere

1. You and all golfers have a common purpose—to play your best game. Considerate and courteous actions set the stage for accomplishing this goal.
2. Good golf requires concentration. Remain quiet when a player is either preparing to play or is playing a shot.
3. Stand quietly and out of range of any player making a stroke. Stand out of any line of play. (The line of play extends from in back of the ball, through the ball, and beyond the target.)
4. Be careful not to disturb players outside your group. For example, the noise of loud talk carries to other parts of the course, thus distracting players in distant areas.
5. Frustrations resulting from hitting unsatisfactory shots or getting bad breaks are not justifications for unpleasant behavior. Complaining, using offensive language, and club throwing are examples of unacceptable actions.

Care of the Golf Course

1. Replace all divots and press them firmly in place. Avoid taking divots with practice swings.
2. Walk carefully on the putting green to avoid marring the surface. Do not step or stand at the edge of the hole. On the practice putting green, stand away from any hole when playing the ball to another cup.

3. Repair ball marks on the putting green. Either with a tee or with a fork-like metal tool (available at golf shops for a nominal cost), lift up and press back the grass around the pit mark, leaving a level surface.
4. After removing the flagstick from the hole, lay it down. Do not drop or throw it on the green.
5. After putting out, lift the ball out of the hole with your hand. Do not twist the putter blade within the cup to retrieve the ball. Such a practice can mar the walls and edges of the hole.
6. Keep all carts (motorized and hand) well away from the greens and aprons and off the teeing grounds. When driving motorized carts, stay on the cart paths as much as possible. Follow the course rules.
7. When leaving a bunker, smooth out the surface so that its condition is as good or better than when you entered it.
8. Do not discard litter on the course. Do your part to maintain the beauty of the golf course.

Playing without Delay

1. Remember—you are one of many golfers paying for the privilege of playing on the course. Play without delay. Follow practices that will help speed up play.
2. If you are new to the game, be ready to play. Have a knowledge of safety, etiquette, and rules, and possess basic skills in the strokes before you attempt to play on the course (see Chapter 9, "Instructions for the New Player").
3. You will need your own set of clubs, a golf bag, balls, and tees. During play, do not borrow clubs from another player.
4. Before starting a round, note the name and number of your golf ball. Also, follow the United States Golf Association (USGA) recommendation of placing a distinguishing mark on the ball so that it can be easily identified without picking it up. If, however, you are unable to see an identifying mark, you may mark and lift the ball, but only after announcing your intention to do so. (A ball lying in a hazard may not be lifted for identification.)
5. Avoid delaying play by taking numerous practice swings. If any practice swings are taken, try to limit the number to one or two.
6. Be ready to play when it is your turn. Planning ahead for some strokes is possible (see chapter 7, "The Putting Stroke").
7. Any instruction should be incidental, if at all. No play should be delayed because one person is attempting to teach another.
8. After you hit a shot, watch the ball and spot its position carefully so that you can walk directly to it. Also, watch the stroke results of other players in your group so that, if necessary, you can help in any ball search.
9. When your ball is on the wrong fairway, permit players playing that hole to have the right-of-way. Avoid interfering with other players. (Before entering another fairway, be sure it is safe to do so.)

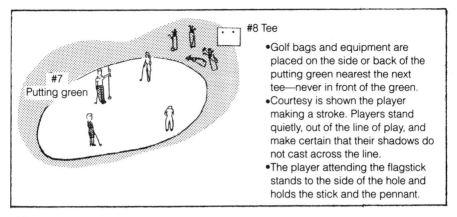

#8 Tee

- Golf bags and equipment are placed on the side or back of the putting green nearest the next tee—never in front of the green.
- Courtesy is shown the player making a stroke. Players stand quietly, out of the line of play, and make certain that their shadows do not cast across the line.
- The player attending the flagstick stands to the side of the hole and holds the stick and the pennant.

Figure 10.1
Etiquette—Putting green.

10. If your group is delaying play by failing to keep its place on the course (falling behind the group ahead by one clear hole), either speed up your play and regain your proper position or invite the players following to play through. Likewise, if your group is searching for a lost ball and holding up play, invite the following group to play through. Wait until the players are out of range before resuming play. (If you are extended the courtesy of playing through, express your appreciation.)

11. At some golf courses on par-3 holes, golfers who have reached the putting green will invite players of the following group to hit their tee shots. While waiting for the group behind to hit their shots, the players on the green should stand off the putting surface, in back of the green, and to one side of the line from the tee to the flagstick.

On the Putting Green

1. Place your golf bag or cart well off and to one side or back of the putting green nearest the next tee (fig. 10.1).

2. Do not step or stand in any line of play. Check your shadow. See that it does not cast in another player's line of putt or over the hole (fig. 10.1).

3. Mark and lift your ball when requested to do so. To mark the ball position, place a small coin or marker behind the ball. If the marker is in another player's line of putt, measure out the necessary putterhead-lengths to one side and move the marker to this spot. (To be certain that the ball is re-placed to its original position, line up the toe of the clubhead with a sta-tionary object before moving the marker.) Follow the same procedure when replacing the ball to its original position (fig. 10.2).

   In stroke play, if a ball lies close to the hole, as after a first putt, the player may putt out rather than mark the ball. This option speeds up play. But never stand in a line of play to hole out.

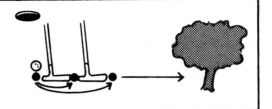

Ball marker interferes with line of putt. After marking ball, line up toe of putter with a stationary object. Measure one or two putterhead-lengths to side. Move marker. Replace in same fashion.

Figure 10.2
Moving ball marker.

4. When attending the flagstick, stand to one side of the hole, at arm's length, and hold the stick and the flag (if within reach). See that your shadow does not cast in the line of play. The stick should be held in the center of the hole until removal is necessary. After removing the flagstick, lay it down where it will not interfere with play. When all players are on the putting green or close to it, a player whose ball lies close to the hole usually offers to attend the flagstick (fig. 10.1).

5. After all players of your group have holed out, be willing to do your part in replacing the flagstick. Leaving this responsibility to the player putting out last indicates a lack of sportsmanship and may delay play.

6. After your group has holed out, replace the flagstick, leave the putting green immediately, and proceed to the next tee. Never remain on the putting green to review play of the hole or to mark scores on the score card. Do not take practice shots that will delay play.

In the Bunker

1. Leave your golf bag or cart well outside the edge of the bunker.
2. Enter the bunker at the lowest bank and take the shortest route to the ball.
3. Before you walk into a bunker to play your shot, check to see whether the rake is nearby. If it is not, secure and place it near you, but where it will not interfere with play. With the rake close at hand, you can rake the sand as you walk from the trap.
4. Avoid entering or standing in a bunker when another golfer is playing from it.
5. On leaving the bunker, rake or in some manner smooth out all footprints and marks, thus leaving the surface of the sand in perfect condition.

Rules

This summary of selected rules is an introduction to your study of the complete rules. It is only a digest and is not a substitute for the official rules as published by the United States Golf Association. (Copies of the rules are available at local golf shops or from the USGA, Far Hills, NJ 07931.)

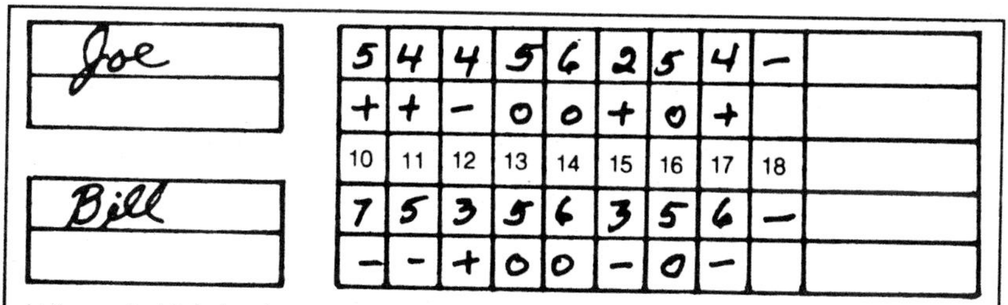

	5	4	4	5	6	2	5	4	—
Joe	+	+	−	o	o	+	o	+	
	10	11	12	13	14	15	16	17	18
Bill	7	5	3	5	6	3	5	6	—
	−	−	+	o	o	−	o	−	

At the end of 9 holes the match between Joe and Bill is all even (all square). Joe wins holes 10 and 11. Joe is 2 holes up. Bill wins hole 12. Joe is 1 hole up; Bill 1 hole down. Holes 13 and 14 are halved (tied). Joe wins hole 15. Hole 16 is halved. Joe is *dormie* 2: he is the same number of holes up as there are holes remaining in the match. Joe wins hole 17, thereby winning the match 3 holes up with 1 hole remaining —3 and 1 or 3-1.

Figure 10.3
Match play score card—last nine holes.

Golfers should have a thorough knowledge of the rules because only then can they play golf properly. To resolve rules, questions that may arise during play, the USGA recommends that all golfers carry rule books as part of their golfing equipment.

Types of Competition

The two main types of golf competition are *stroke play* and *match play*. In stroke play, the person with the lowest score for the stipulated number of rounds, usually four rounds (72 holes), is the winner. If two or more players are tied for first place at the end of a tournament, these players either play an 18-hole round, or they play one or more extra holes, and the first player to make the low score on a hole is the winner. (The committee in charge determines the method of playing off ties in tournaments.) In stroke competition, all players are properly referred to as *competitors*, except that, within a playing group, the contestants are called *fellow-competitors*.

Match play competition is based on the number of holes won, not the total score for a round. In a single match, a player competes against only one other player, the *opponent*. They play until one person is more holes ahead than there are holes remaining to be played in the match. If the match is tied at the end of the stipulated round, players usually continue play until one player wins a hole. Match play is an elimination-type tournament, so in the final round, only two players remain to compete for the championship.

Rules for Teeing Off

1. Play is started at each hole by teeing the ball within the teeing ground. This area, two club-lengths in depth, is bounded in the front and on the sides by the outer edges of the tee markers.

2. Honor, the privilege of teeing first, is usually decided by lot on the first tee. After the first hole, honor is decided by scores on the previous hole. The person with the lowest score shoots first, and the others follow according to their scores. If two or more players score the same on a hole, they tee off in the order they followed on the previous tee.

3. The ball is in play after a stroke is made from the tee. If a player, in addressing the ball not yet in play, accidentally knocks the ball off the tee, it may be teed again without penalty.

4. If a player swings at and misses the ball on the tee, the stroke counts—the ball is in play. No ball is in play if the tee shot is lost or hit out of bounds, or, in stroke play, when the competitor plays the ball from outside the teeing ground.

General Rules

1. After teeing off, the players continue to strike the ball, in turn, until they hole out. The ball should be played as it lies and not be touched except to strike it, unless situations or rules permit or require otherwise.

2. The ball farthest from the hole is played first. (Except in stroke play, the player may putt out instead of marking a ball.)

3. Any attempt to hit the ball is counted as a stroke, whether or not the ball is struck.

4. When the ball is in play, the player may *not* press or stamp down ground, or break, bend, or remove anything fixed or growing. However, the surface on the teeing ground being played may be improved.

5. If, after addressing the ball in play, the ball moves, the penalty is one stroke, and the ball must be replaced.

   When a player accidentally moves a ball in searching for it in such areas as casual water, ground under repair, or a hole or runway made by a burrowing animal, the ball is replaced without penalty, unless the player elects to take relief from the situation.

6. Loose impediments, such as fallen leaves, pebbles, worms, and insects that interfere with play, may be moved. If a ball lies in a hazard, however, loose impediments may *not* be touched or moved.

   Through the green, if after moving a loose impediment within one club-length of the ball, the ball moves before the player has played it, the penalty is one stroke and the ball must be replaced. (Through the green is all of the course except all hazards and the teeing ground and putting green of the hole being played.)

7. In certain situations, a player may lift or be required to lift a ball and place or drop it.

   To drop a ball, a player stands erect, facing any direction, holds the ball at shoulder height with the arm extended, and drops the ball. The ball must be dropped in an area prescribed by the rule involved. For instance, when taking relief from a cart path, the ball is dropped within

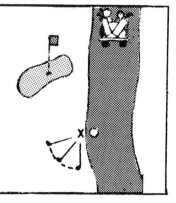

Nearest point of relief for right-handed player is *X*. Place marker (tee or ball marker) at *X* and measure one club-length with any club. Drop ball within drop area, not nearer the hole, without penalty.

Figure 10.4
Ball on paved cart path (no interference to stance or swing).

one club-length of the nearest point of relief, not nearer the hole, without penalty (fig. 10.4).

8. When a ball lies on the wrong putting green, the ball must be lifted and dropped off the putting green within one club-length of the nearest point of relief, not nearer the hole and not in a hazard, without penalty.

9. *Movable obstructions,* such as water hoses, rakes, trash containers, and benches that interfere with play, may be moved.

    If a player moves such an obstruction and the ball moves, the ball must be replaced without penalty.

10. *Immovable obstructions* include paved cart paths, shelters, and sprinkler heads. (Note that walls, fences, stakes, and railings defining out of bounds are not obstructions. No relief is allowed without penalty.)

    Through the green, if a ball lies in or on an immovable obstruction or if the obstruction interferes with the player's stance or swing, the ball may be lifted and dropped within one club-length of the nearest point of relief without penalty.

    If an immovable obstruction interferes with play in a bunker, the ball must be dropped in the bunker. If on the putting green, the already stated conditions exist, or if the obstruction is situated between the ball on the putting green and the hole, the ball may be lifted and placed at the nearest point of relief without penalty. In a water hazard, no relief is allowed without penalty.

11. Through the green, if a ball lies in casual water (a temporary accumulation of water) or if the casual water interferes with the player's stance or swing, the ball may be lifted and dropped within one club-length of the nearest point of relief, not nearer the hole, without penalty.

    If a ball lies in casual water in a bunker, the ball must be dropped in the bunker, not nearer the hole, without penalty, or dropped outside the bunker with a penalty of one stroke. (See line of drop in the sections "Rules for Hazards" and "Unplayable Ball" later in the chapter.)

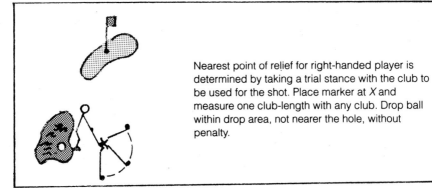

Nearest point of relief for right-handed player is determined by taking a trial stance with the club to be used for the shot. Place marker at X and measure one club-length with any club. Drop ball within drop area, not nearer the hole, without penalty.

Figure 10.5
Ball in casual water (interference to stance).

If on the putting green the already stated conditions exist, or if the casual water is between the ball on the putting green and the hole, the ball may be lifted and placed, not nearer the hole, without penalty.

The rule for relief from casual water also applies to such situations as ground under repair, and a hole, runway, or cast made by a burrowing animal. Except when the ball lies in a water hazard, no relief is allowed from a hole, runway, or cast made by a burrowing animal.

Note: Procedures for determining the nearest point of relief for immovable obstructions and from such areas as ground under repair and casual water are the same (figs. 10.4, 10.5).

12. In stroke play, the penalty for playing a wrong ball, except from a hazard, is two strokes. The player must then play the correct ball. The strokes played with the wrong ball are not counted in the score.

    In match play, the penalty for playing a wrong ball, except from a hazard, is loss of hole. Any strokes played with a wrong ball from a hazard are not counted in the player's score.

13. If another player's ball interferes with your play, you may request that the ball be marked and lifted.

14. You may ask only your caddie, partner, or partner's caddie for advice.

15. The general penalty for breaking a rule in stroke play is two strokes; in match play, loss of hole. For example: If a player stamps down the grass in back of a ball lying on the fairway, the penalty in stroke play is two strokes and loss of hole in match play.

16. The score card should be checked for local rules and interpretations that apply to the course being played.

Rules for the Putting Green

1. Taking a stance with either foot touching or astride the line of putt is prohibited. The line extends from the hole to a point beyond the ball. Penalty for breach of the rule is two strokes in stroke play and loss of hole in match play.

2. When playing the ball from the putting green, request that the flagstick be attended or removed from the hole. The penalty for playing a ball from the green and having it strike the flagstick is two strokes in stroke play and loss of hole in match play.

3. In stroke play, if a ball played from the putting green strikes a fellow-competitor's ball (also on the putting green), the penalty is two strokes. If the fellow-competitor's ball is moved by the impact, it must be replaced.

   In match play, there is no penalty for a player's ball played from the putting green striking the opponent's ball, also on the green. If the opponent's ball is moved by the impact, it must be replaced.

4. When the ball lies on the putting green, it may be marked, lifted, and cleaned.

5. Sand and loose soil are considered loose impediments on the putting green only. They may be picked up or brushed aside with the hand or club. If the ball is accidentally moved in removing loose impediments on the green, it is replaced without penalty.

6. When any part of the ball overhangs the hole, the player, after walking to the hole without delay, may wait ten seconds. If the ball does not fall into the hole in that time, it is considered to be at rest.

   Breach of the ten-second rule: if after the ten-second period, a ball lying two on the edge of the hole falls into the cup, the player's score for the hole is 2 plus one penalty stroke—a 3.

Rules for Hazards

1. By USGA definition, hazards are bunkers and water hazards (including lateral water hazards). A bunker is usually a depressed area of bare ground covered with sand, frequently called a sand trap, but correctly referred to as a bunker. Grass-covered areas within or surrounding the bunker are not parts of the hazard.

   The limits of water hazards are usually defined by stakes or lines: yellow for water hazards and red for lateral water hazards. Marked boundaries (lines and stakes) are within the hazards. The grass-covered areas or any dry ground within the indicated margins of the water hazard are part of the hazard.

2. When the ball lies in a hazard, loose impediments may not be touched or moved.

3. Man-made objects, such as rakes, may be moved.

4. In addressing the ball in a hazard, you may *not* ground the club. The surface of the hazard cannot be touched before taking the forward swing to strike the ball.

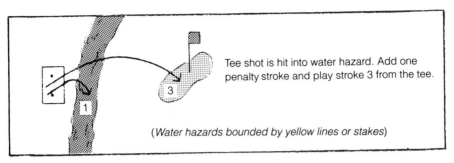

Tee shot is hit into water hazard. Add one penalty stroke and play stroke 3 from the tee.

(Water hazards bounded by yellow lines or stakes)

Figure 10.6
Water hazard—Option A.

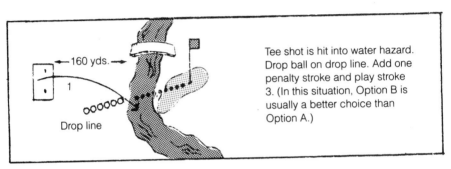

Tee shot is hit into water hazard. Drop ball on drop line. Add one penalty stroke and play stroke 3. (In this situation, Option B is usually a better choice than Option A.)

Figure 10.7
Water hazard—Option B.

5. Water hazard: If a ball is lost in a water hazard or declared impossible to play, the player may proceed under one of two options:
   A. Drop a ball under penalty of one stroke at the spot from which the original ball was played. If the original ball was played from the tee, the ball may be teed anywhere on the teeing ground (fig. 10.6).
   B. Drop a ball under penalty of one stroke any distance behind the hazard, keeping the point at which the ball last crossed the hazard margin between the hole and the spot on which the ball is dropped (fig. 10.7).
6. Lateral water hazard: If a ball is lost in a lateral water hazard or declared impossible to play, the player may choose one of three options to continue play (Options A and B are the same for both water and lateral water hazards):
   A. Drop a ball under penalty of one stroke at the spot from which the original ball was played. If the ball was played from the tee, the ball may be teed anywhere on the teeing ground (fig. 10.8).
   B. Drop a ball under penalty of one stroke any distance behind the hazard, keeping the point at which the ball last crossed the hazard margin between the hole and the spot on which the ball is dropped (fig. 10.9).

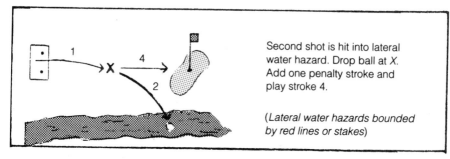

Figure 10.8
Lateral water hazard—Option A.

Second shot is hit into lateral water hazard. Drop ball at *X*. Add one penalty stroke and play stroke 4.

(*Lateral water hazards bounded by red lines or stakes*)

Figure 10.9
Lateral water hazard—Option B.

Tee shot is hit into lateral water hazard. Drop ball on drop line. Add one penalty stroke and play stroke 3.

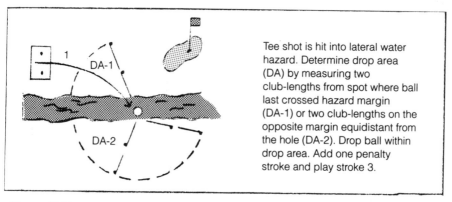

Figure 10.10
Lateral water hazard—Option C.

Tee shot is hit into lateral water hazard. Determine drop area (DA) by measuring two club-lengths from spot where ball last crossed hazard margin (DA-1) or two club-lengths on the opposite margin equidistant from the hole (DA-2). Drop ball within drop area. Add one penalty stroke and play stroke 3.

C. Under penalty of one stroke, drop a ball within two club-lengths of where the ball last crossed the margin of the hazard or within two club-lengths of a point equidistant from the hole on the opposite margin of the hazard (fig. 10.10).

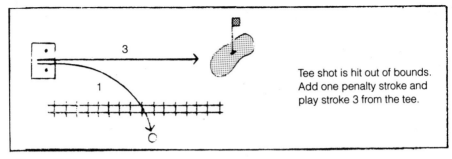

Figure 10.11
Ball out of bounds.

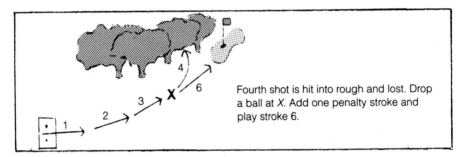

Figure 10.12
Lost ball.

Ball Out of Bounds

A ball is out of bounds when (1) all of it lies beyond the inside points of the out-of-bounds stakes or fence or (2) all of the ball lies on or beyond a line chalked to indicate out of bounds.

The penalty for hitting a ball out of bounds is one stroke, and the player loses the distance of the shot. The player plays again from where the original ball was played and adds one penalty stroke (fig. 10.11).

Lost Ball

A player is allowed five minutes to search for a ball. After that time, the ball is considered lost.

The penalty for a ball lost outside of a water hazard is one stroke and loss of distance (the same penalty as for out of bounds) (fig. 10.12).

Provisional Ball

When a ball is hit that may be out of bounds or lost outside of a water hazard, a provisional ball may be played. For example, suppose you hit a long drive from the tee toward an out-of-bounds fence. From the distant view, it is uncertain whether the ball is in bounds or out of bounds. After informing your playing companions of your intention, you may hit a provisional ball. If the original ball is in bounds, play it and pick up the provisional ball; if the original ball is out of bounds, play the provisional ball. Stroke and distance penalty applies.

Playing a provisional ball for one that may be out of bounds or lost (outside of a water hazard) saves the player the time and trouble of returning to the original spot of play to hit another ball. The provisional ball may be played up to the spot where the original ball may be lost or out of bounds.

Unplayable Ball

A ball may be declared unplayable at any place on the course, except in a water hazard. The player is the sole judge as to when a ball is unplayable.

For example, a ball is likely to be declared unplayable when it is lying against a tree, a large, embedded rock, or an out-of-bounds fence.

When the ball is declared unplayable, the player may proceed under any one of three options:

A. Play the next stroke at the spot from which the original ball was played, under penalty of one stroke (stroke and distance penalty) (fig. 10.13).
B. Drop a ball within two club-lengths of the unplayable position, not nearer the hole, under penalty of one stroke (fig. 10.14).
C. Drop a ball any distance behind the unplayable position—keeping that point between the hole and the spot on which the ball is dropped, under penalty of one stroke (fig. 10.15).

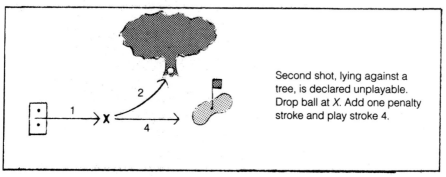

Second shot, lying against a tree, is declared unplayable. Drop ball at X. Add one penalty stroke and play stroke 4.

Figure 10.13
Unplayable ball—Option A.

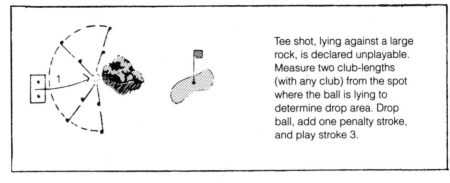

Tee shot, lying against a large rock, is declared unplayable. Measure two club-lengths (with any club) from the spot where the ball is lying to determine drop area. Drop ball, add one penalty stroke, and play stroke 3.

Figure 10.14
Unplayable ball—Option B.

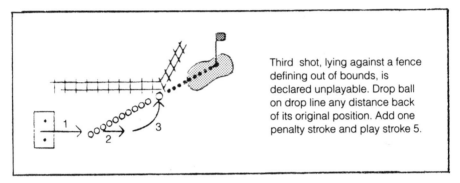

Third shot, lying against a fence defining out of bounds, is declared unplayable. Drop ball on drop line any distance back of its original position. Add one penalty stroke and play stroke 5.

Figure 10.15
Unplayable ball—Option C.

Handicaps

A handicap is a number representing a golfer's playing ability. Most players score above par for 18-hole rounds; their course handicaps, which may range from 1 to 40 and above, indicate the approximate number of strokes they shoot over par. A player with a handicap of 0 averages near par and is called a scratch golfer. The few players averaging near and below par have plus handicaps.

The USGA Handicap System provides a method of establishing course handicaps, thereby ensuring fair competition—on any course—among players of different abilities. A *handicap index,* based on a player's lowest ten of the last twenty scores, is calculated by a club or association. This index number can then be converted to a course handicap by using the USGA conversion tables posted at most courses. Thus, golfers with handicap indexes can simply check the figures on the charts to find their course handicaps. For example, a golfer with a handicap index of 18.6 plays a course rated 100. The handicap on the chart reads 16. When this golfer plays a more difficult course, rated 135, the handicap changes to 22.

Handicaps equalize competitive play. In an 18-hole stroke event, a net score is computed for each player by subtracting the player's handicap from the actual (gross) score.

In match play, the golfer with the higher handicap is allowed to subtract strokes from certain holes. For example, two opponents have handicaps of 7 and 4. The player with the 7-handicap subtracts one stroke from each of the scores on the holes with handicap ratings of 1, 2, and 3. On the score card (fig. 1.2), the three holes rated most difficult on the White and Blue courses are 5, 10, and 8; on the Red course, 5, 14, and 1. The player with a 4-handicap gives the opponent with a 7-handicap one stroke on each of these holes.

To maintain a correct and up-to-date handicap index, players must report all scores as per USGA regulations. (For complete and exact information on handicaps, see the *USGA Handicap System and Golf Committee Manual*.)

Selection of Accessories and Equipment

Comfortable and appropriate sports clothes should be worn for golf. Complete lines of attractive golf clothes for men and women are sold in many stores and course golf shops. Some golf courses have rather strict dress codes. You might want to check on such regulations before visiting a new club or course.

The preferred shoes for playing are golf shoes with spikes or with some kind of "traction" soles. They will help you to maintain your balance in swinging and also will make walking on the course easy. Low-heeled shoes must always be worn on the course. Many players wear either a glove on the left hand or gloves on both hands. Gloves may be an aid in holding the club or in preventing blisters or calluses from forming on the hands. Wearing a hat or visor provides protection from the sun.

If you plan to walk the course and carry your clubs, choose a lightweight bag with good balance. A variety of golf bags is available. Select one that best suits your needs. Hand carts are popular accessory items. Hand carts and motorized carts can be rented at most courses.

Golf balls vary in compression. For the expert, long-hitting player, a high-compression ball (rated near 100) is preferred. Average golfers find lower compression balls more suitable to their games. Balls with cut-resistant covers are favored by many players.

Choose a putter that you like. Most golf shops will allow you to use and test putters on a practice putting green or on an indoor putting mat. A selection can be made from a wide variety of new and used putters.

In selecting irons and woods, choose clubs that fit you because, with them, you can play your best golf. Your strength, body build, and swing are some factors to consider in proper fitting. Before buying any clubs, talk with one or more golf professionals or trained salespersons and have them check your swing. They can then make a judgment as to what clubs suit you best. These services are free.

Golf shops offer players a great variety of matched sets of clubs in different styles and costs; some shops carry suitable used sets. For beginning golfers and some novices, starter sets consisting of seven or fewer clubs are adequate: A typical seven-club set includes the 3-, 5-, 7-, and 9-irons, the 1- and 3- or (4, 5)-woods, and putter. Playing with fewer clubs makes the game less complicated and does not deter progress in developing skill.

Because of the differences in height, strength, and hand size between men and women, clubs differ in club shaft flexibility, grip size, and weight. For the average man golfer, the R-shaft (regular) is the best choice; for average women golfers, the L-shaft is best. Players with above-average power and strength may choose clubs with stiffer shafts, while golfers with less-than-average strength may be helped by more flexible shafts.

Total weight and swingweight are considered in fitting clubs. Simply stated, swingweight is a measurement of the clubhead weight in proportion to the shaft and grip weight. This proportional relationship is an important factor in the "feel" and balance of the club, as is the flex of the shaft during the swing. In general, the swingweight of women's clubs ranges from C-0 to C-9; in men's clubs, swingweight is D-0 and above.

Much experimentation, testing, and research are being done to produce clubs that offer more accuracy and greater distance. New designs and new construction materials continue to be introduced into the golf club market. Your best source of information on current developments in club technology is your golf professional.

Review

1. Distinguish between stroke play and match play. If player A wins a round over player B in match play, is it possible that A could have lost the round had the competition been stroke play?
2. What rule options does a player have in the following situations: a ball is lost in a water hazard; a ball is lost in a lateral water hazard; a ball is lying in a tree trunk and is impossible to play; a ball is lost in the rough?
3. How should you mark and lift your ball if it lies in another player's line of putt? What is the proper way to attend the flagstick?
4. Some players mistakenly state that the penalty for hitting a ball out of bounds is two strokes. What is the difference between a two-stroke penalty and the stroke and distance penalty? What are some examples of rule violations that incur a two-stroke penalty?
5. State at least six points of etiquette that players should observe to help keep the course in good condition. State at least five points of etiquette to be observed on the putting green.

An Afterword—You and the Game of Golf

Nearly 100 years ago, a British writer and golfer said that he would like to see an Act of Parliament that would make it compulsory for every player to take a thorough examination on the golf rules. We might wonder what this gentleman would say about some of today's golfers!

Fortunately, most players do show respect: respect for the game, respect for other players, and respect for the course. But unfortunately, some players do not. They fail to observe the golf rules and play only a version of the game. They neglect to follow the rules of etiquette; they detract from the pleasures and amenities of the fellowship of golf. Because of their slow play, they prevent more people from participating in the game. They leave the course in poor condition. They discard litter. They fail to follow simple practices that help to keep the course in good condition.

While a law requiring every player to be respectful cannot be enacted, we can all make a contribution to golf by upholding and preserving the rules and traditions of this venerable game. It is hoped that readers of this book will be proud to number themselves among the majority of golfers—those with class and consideration.

A Golfer's Code

> - Accept and meet the challenges of the game.
> - Play by the rules. The rules are self-enforced.
> - Be aware of sharing the course with other players. Play without delay, keeping your place on the course and not holding up the play of golfers following.
> - Observe the safety precautions and the rules of etiquette to the finest degree.
> - Appreciate the course and do your part in helping to maintain its beauty.

May your actions show your appreciation of the game and contribute to the recreation and pleasure of all golfers. May your participation in this fine pastime be one of success and pleasure.

Glossary

Ace
A hole-in-one.

Addressing the ball
Taking the stance and grounding the club, except that, in a hazard, the club may *not* be grounded.

All square
A term used in match play to indicate that the match is tied.

Approach shot
A stroke played to the putting green.

Apron
The area surrounding the putting green.

Away
The ball lying farthest from the hole.

Back 9
The last nine holes of an 18-hole course. Also called "in 9."

Backspin
A reverse spin of the ball in the vertical plane.

Banana ball
A slice.

Barranca
A deep ravine. (Spanish)

Birdie
A score of 1 under par for a hole.

Bite
The backspin on the ball that causes the ball to stop upon landing on the ground.

Bogey
A term commonly used to describe a score of 1 over par for a hole.

Brassie
The 2-wood.

Break of green
The slant or slope of the putting green.

Bunker
A hazard—usually, a depressed area covered with sand.

Caddie

A person who carries the clubs and otherwise assists a player as the rules provide.

Casual water

A temporary accumulation of water, except in a water hazard.

Chip shot

A short, low shot played to the putting green. Also called a run-up shot.

Course rating

A number representing the playing difficulty of a course for scratch players.

Cup

The term commonly used for the hole on the putting green.

Curtis Cup Matches

Competition between women amateur golfers. One team from the United States plays against a team made up of players from England, Scotland, Wales, Northern Ireland, and Ireland.

Divot

A piece of turf cut or displaced in making a stroke. Should be replaced and pressed down.

Dogleg

A hole in which the fairway curves to the right or left.

Dormie

A term used in match play. A player is dormie when he or she is as many holes up as there are holes remaining to be played.

Double bogey

A term commonly used to describe a score of 2 over par for a hole.

Double eagle

A score of 3 under par for a hole.

Draw

A shot that curves slightly in flight from right to left.

Driver

The 1-wood.

Dub

An unskilled golfer. Also means to hit a poor shot.

Duffer

A player with poor skill.

Eagle

A score of 2 under par for a hole.

"Explosion" shot

A shot played from a bunker. An attempt is made to swing the club through the sand well back of the ball.

Fade

A shot that curves slightly in flight from left to right.

Fairway
The closely mowed grassy area between the tee and putting green.

Fat shot
A shot in which the ground is struck before contacting the ball, usually resulting in a poor shot.

Fellow-competitor
In stroke play, any person with whom the competitor plays.

Flagstick
The marker that indicates the location of the hole.

Flat swing
A swing in which the club is swung in a low arc. At the top of the backswing, the horizontal position of the club shaft is lower than in the average swing.

Flub
A poorly hit shot. Also means to hit a poor shot.

Fore!
A warning cry to anyone who might be endangered by a golf shot.

Forecaddie
Appointed by tournament committees, forecaddies are stationed on the course to watch oncoming shots and to point out the location where balls have come to rest.

Foursome
Four players playing together who may or may not be engaged in a match.

Frog hair
The grass surrounding the putting green.

Front 9
The first nine holes of an 18-hole course. Also called "out 9."

Gross score
The actual total score for a round.

Grounding the club
Placing the sole of the club on the ground in preparation for making the stroke. Illegal in hazards.

Ground under repair
Staked or lined area on which work is being done. A ball coming to rest in such an area may be lifted and dropped in accordance with the rules.

Halved or halving a hole
In match play, to tie a hole.

Handicap
Simply stated, a number representing a player's scoring ability. Handicap stroke allowances equalize players of different abilities.

Hazard
By USGA definitions, bunkers and water hazards.

High handicapper
A player who shoots many strokes over par. An unskilled player.

Hole

(1) The receptacle on the putting green that is 4 1/4 inches in diameter and at least 4 inches deep. (2) One unit or division of the course.

Hole high

When the ball is in a position as far as the hole but off to either side of it.

Hole out

To complete the play of a hole.

Honor

The privilege of hitting first from the tee.

Hook

A shot that curves in flight to the left due to a horizontal, counterclockwise spin on the ball.

In 9

The second nine holes of an 18-hole course. Also called "back 9."

Lateral water hazard

A water hazard running approximately parallel to the line of play. Marked by red stakes or lines.

Lie

The position of the ball on the ground.

Links

A golf course, usually one located along a seaside.

Loft of club

The angle of pitch of the clubface.

Loose impediments

Objects such as dead grass and fallen leaves, pebbles, worms, fallen twigs.

Low handicapper

A skilled golfer who shoots near par.

LPGA

Ladies Professional Golf Association.

Mashie

In the past, the 5-iron was called the mashie.

Medalist

The player with the lowest score for a qualifying round of a match play tournament.

Medal play

More commonly called stroke play. Competition by total score.

Metal woods

"Wood" clubs with clubheads constructed of metal, such as stainless steel or graphite.

Mid-iron

Term formerly used to designate a 2-iron.

Mixed foursome

A group of four players made up of two women and two men.

Mulligan

An illegal practice of taking a second drive from the first tee without penalty if the first shot is a poor one.

Nassau scoring system

A system of scoring allowing one point to the winner of each nine holes and one point for the match.

Net score

The score after subtracting the handicap from the gross score.

Niblick

A colorful term to designate a high-lofted iron, such as a 9-iron.

Obstruction

An artificial object on the course that may be movable or fixed.

On the beach

In the sand or a bunker.

Open tournament

A competitive event in which both amateurs and professionals play, such as the United States Open Championship and The Open Championship of the British Isles.

Opponent

The player opposing you in a match.

Out 9

The first nine holes of an 18-hole course. Also called ''front 9.''

Out of bounds

Ground on which play is prohibited. Usually marked by out-of-bounds stakes or fences.

Par

An arbitrary standard of scoring excellence based on the length of a hole and allowing two putts on the putting green. (The difficulty of a hole may also be considered in setting par.)

PGA

Professional Golfers' Association of America.

Pin high

Same as *hole high.*

Pitch shot

A shot that travels in a high trajectory played to the putting green.

Press

Attempting to hit the ball beyond your normal power.

Pronation

An anatomical term to describe the turning of the hand and forearm inward. Supination is the opposite action, in which the hand and forearm are turned out so that the palm is facing up.

Provisional ball

A second ball played when the first ball played is or is thought to be out of bounds or lost outside a water hazard.

Pull
A shot that travels in a straight line, but to the left of the intended target.

Push
A shot that travels in a straight line, but to the right of the intended target.

Quail high
Low-flying shot.

Rainmaker
Shot with a very high trajectory.

Rough
The areas bordering the fairway in which the grass, weeds, and so on are allowed to grow freely.

Royal and Ancient Golf Club of St. Andrews, Scotland (The R and A)
The governing body of golf in Great Britain.

Rub of the green
An unpredictable happening to the ball when the ball in motion or at rest is stopped or deflected by an outside agency.

Ryder Cup Matches
Competition between two men's professional teams: the Great Britain and Europe team matched against the U.S. team.

Sand trap
Term used in place of the correct word *bunker*. See *Bunker*.

Scotch foursome
A match in which partners compete. Each partnership of two plays alternate strokes using one ball.

Scratch player
A player who has a handicap of 0, shooting consistently near par.

Slice
A shot that curves in flight to the right, due to a horizontal, clockwise spin on the ball.

Slope rating
A number representing the comparative difficulty of courses in relation to players with handicaps above scratch.

Socket
The part of the clubhead into which the shaft is fitted. Also called *neck* or *hosel*.

Spoon
The 3-wood.

Stance
The position of the feet in addressing the ball.

Stroke play
Competition by total strokes.

Stymie

To have another player's golf ball or some object blocking your line of play. Also refers to an obsolete rule of golf.

Summer rules

Term used to describe play disallowing "winter rules." Ball is played as it lies unless rules allow relief.

Tee

The starting area for a hole. Also, the peg on which the ball is placed for driving.

Teeing ground

The exact area from which play is started at each hole. This area, two club-lengths in depth, is bounded in front and on the sides by the outer edges of the tee markers.

Tee markers

The markers placed on the tee to indicate the forward limits of the teeing area.

Texas wedge

A name applied to the putter when it is used to play any shot from off the putting green.

Through the green

Refers to the whole of the course, except the teeing ground and putting green of the hole being played and all hazards.

Underclubbing

A frequent judgment error made by players who use a club with less distance potential than required. Thus, the ball comes to rest short of the putting green. Overclubbing errors are less common.

Up and down

Holing out in two strokes from off the green.

Upright swing

A swing in which the club is swung high into the air on the backswing and follow-through. The opposite of a flat swing.

USGA

The United States Golf Association, the governing body of golf in the United States.

Walker Cup Matches

Competition between men amateur golfers. One team from the United States plays against a team made up of players from England, Scotland, Wales, Northern Ireland, and Ireland.

Water hazard

A water hazard usually running across the fairway, thus making it possible to drop a ball behind the hazard according to the rules. Marked by yellow stakes or lines.

Whiff

To swing at the ball and miss it completely. To fan the ball.

Winter rules

Special local rules that permit the ball to be moved to a better lie on the fairway. Also called "preferred lies."

Rules Test and Answers

Rule Decisions

Give the correct ruling for the following situations as follows: for No Penalty, *NP;* 2-Stroke Penalty, *2SP;* 1-Stroke Penalty, *1SP;* Disqualification, *D;* Loss of Hole, *LH;* Stroke and Distance, *SD.*

Questions referring only to match play are so noted. Sample: *Match play.* Before playing a stroke on the putting green, A tests the surface by rolling a ball across the green. (Answer: *LH.*)

When no type of competition is indicated, assume that the question refers to stroke play or that the rule decision is the same for both stroke and match play. Sample: Before playing a stroke from the putting green, A, in using his hand to brush a fly off the ball, accidentally moves the ball. (Answer: *NP;* must replace ball.)

1. Before starting their round, fellow-competitors A and B decide to concede putts less than 1 foot in length.
2. To speed up their play, A and B agree that they will take no more than one practice swing before each shot.
3. *Match play.* A stamps down the surface in his line of putt.
4. On the fairway, B pulls out a dandelion that interferes with her backswing.
5. After playing the fifth hole, B practices putting on the putting green and delays the play of her group.
6. *Match play.* B delays play at the fifth hole and before teeing off on the sixth hole.
7. A takes two practice swings in the bunker without touching the sand; however, he does touch a mound of grass-covered ground with the clubhead.
8. *Match play.* During play of a hole, B plays a practice shot to the putting green.
9. While waiting on the fairway for slow players ahead, A hits a few practice shots with a plastic practice ball.
10. B's ball lies on the putting green. While waiting for her fellow-competitors to shoot onto the green, B drops a ball on the apron of the green and takes a practice putt.

11. After completing play on the second hole, A drops a ball into the bunker and plays a practice shot, without any delay of play.
12. After A and B have hit their tee shots on a par-3 hole, A asks B what club she used for her tee shot.
13. *Match play.* While A is considering whether or not to hit a ball lying close to an out-of-bounds fence, B, his opponent, suggests that A go ahead and try to hit the ball.
14. A's ball lies 130 yards from the green; B's ball lies 128 yards from the green. B carefully watches what club A selects for his shot.
15. A places a club on the ground to align his stance. Before hitting his shot, he picks up the club.
16. B is playing a putt from off the putting green. Her caddie touches a spot on the green to indicate a point of aim.
17. Before A plays a putt on the green, his caddie points out the correct line of play by touching a spot on the putting green with the flagstick.
18. Players are waiting to tee off on the third hole. On the second hole, A topped three wood shots on the fairway. A asks B for advice. B suggests that A swing slower.
19. A has the honor, but B tees off first.
20. B plays an approach shot to the green out of turn.
21. *Match play.* A's ball is farther from the hole than B's ball; however, B shoots first.
22. After teeing the ball on the teeing ground, A stamps down the turf back of the ball. Then, in addressing the ball, he accidentally knocks it off the tee.
23. B swings at her tee shot and misses the ball. She then stamps down the grass back of the ball.
24. B hits her tee shot out of bounds. She tees another ball and accidentally knocks it off the tee.
25. With the ball teed outside the teeing ground, B hits a drive 200 yards down the center of the fairway.
26. A swings at his first shot from the teeing ground and misses the ball. In addressing the ball again, he accidentally knocks it off the tee.
27. A's ball is partially buried on the rough. He tells B, his fellow-competitor, of his intention to lift the ball for identification, thus allowing B to observe the marking, lifting, and replacing of the ball.
28. A's ball is partially buried in the sand of a bunker. After following the rule of announcing his intention to lift the ball, he marks and lifts it for identification.
29. *Match play.* B accidentally touches the sand in a bunker as she addresses the ball.
30. B's ball is lying on an island of grass-covered ground in a bunker. In addressing the ball, she grounds the club.
31. An out-of-bounds stake interferes with B's backswing. She removes the stake.

32. Before walking into a bunker to play a shot, A takes a practice swing and accidentally hits a dead twig into the bunker and it lands behind the ball. He removes the dead twig before playing his shot.

33. In taking her backswing to play a shot from a bunker, B accidentally touches a leaf lying on the sand.

34. *Match play.* Before playing a shot from under a tree, B carefully entwines one branch with another, without damaging the tree.

35. *Match play.* A plays a wrong ball from a lateral water hazard and then plays the correct ball.

36. B plays a wrong ball from a bunker and then discovers her mistake. She then plays the correct ball.

37. *Match play.* In a match between A and B, A plays a wrong ball from the fairway.

38. A plays a wrong ball from the rough and then discovers his mistake. He then plays the correct ball.

39. B's ball lies on the putting green. Before putting, she brushes away sand in her line of putt with her foot.

40. *Match play.* On the putting green, A stands astride his line of play to putt the ball.

41. In brushing away sand in her line of putt with the clubhead, B accidentally moves the ball.

42. A's ball lies 5 feet off the putting green. Before playing his shot to the green, he repairs ball and spike marks in his line of play.

43. Before putting the ball lying on the putting green, B brushes dew out of her line of play with the clubhead.

44. *Match play.* A concedes a putt to his opponent by hitting the ball to B.

45. A's ball lies 3 feet off the putting green. He strokes the ball, and it strikes the unattended flagstick.

46. B's ball lies 3 feet off the putting green. She strokes the ball, and it strikes the attended flagstick.

47. *Match play.* A strokes a ball from the putting green, and it strikes the flagstick attended by his opponent's (B's) caddie.

48. In playing a shot up a hill to the putting green, B is unable to see the flagstick. Her caddie holds up the flagstick to indicate the position of the hole.

49. In helping A search for a ball, fellow-competitor B accidentally moves the ball.

50. A lifts a twig near his ball lying on the putting green. In so doing, he accidentally moves the ball.

51. B hits her drive into a fairway hillside. As she addresses the ball, it moves and rolls 5 feet down the hill.

52. On a par-3 hole, A and B have both reached the putting green with their tee shots. A putts, and his ball strikes and knocks B's ball into the hole.

53. *Match play.* A strokes his ball on the putting green, and it strikes and moves the ball of his opponent, B.

54. A's ball lies a few inches off the putting green. He putts, and the ball strikes and moves B's ball lying on the putting green.

55. After lifting his ball from the putting green, A places a marker in the correct position on the green.

56. After lifting a ball from casual water in a bunker, B tosses the ball to a spot in the bunker, free of casual and not nearer the hole, and continues play.

57. On the fairway, A moves a loose impediment lying within one club-length of the ball, and the ball moves before he addresses it.

58. On the fairway, loose soil lies behind B's ball. She brushes away the soil with her hand.

59. In the rough, A lifts some dead twigs and pebbles lying behind the ball.

60. In moving a rake from a grassy slope outside a bunker, A accidentally moves the ball.

61. B's ball lies in the rough close to the fairway. An immovable obstruction interferes with her stance. After determining the nearest point of relief, she drops the ball on the fairway within the one club-length area. She proceeds to play the ball.

62. A drain pipe in a bunker interferes with B's swing. She drops a ball outside the bunker on the correct drop line, not nearer the hole, and plays the shot.

63. A's ball comes to rest in a bunker completely filled with casual water. He drops a ball outside the hazard, keeping the point where the ball originally lay between the hole and the spot on which he drops the ball.

64. Casual water intervenes between B's ball, lying on the putting green, and the hole. She lifts and places the ball at the nearest point of relief, not nearer the hole.

65. *Match play.* A's ball lies 10 feet off the putting green. Casual water on the putting green intervenes between the ball and the hole. He lifts the ball and drops it, no nearer the hole, but avoiding interference of the casual water, and continues play.

66. A lifts his ball from the wrong putting green. He measures two club-lengths from the correct point off the green and drops the ball. Deciding he is in error, he lifts the ball and drops it within one club-length from the proper point.

67. B hits her ball into casual water in a bunker. She drops the ball in the bunker within one club-length of the nearest point of relief, not nearer the hole.

68. A, in taking a practice swing in a grassy area within the boundaries of a water hazard, digs a divot from the ground.

69. B hits her tee shot into the middle of a lake. She shoots again from the tee.

70. A hits his third shot from a position 200 yards (spot X) from the hole. After searching the time limit, he declares the ball to be lost.

71. B hits her tee shot out of bounds.

72. A stands out of bounds to hit a ball lying in bounds.

73. B believes that her drive into deep rough may be lost. With no mention of her intention, she tees another ball and hits it into the middle of the fairway.
74. A declares his ball unplayable in a bunker. He takes the option of dropping the ball in the bunker within two club-lengths of the unplayable position, not nearer the hole.
75. B sees her tee shot come to rest against a large tree in the middle of the fairway. Believing that the ball may be unplayable, she announces her intention to play a provisional ball and proceeds to do so.

Score Computations

A. On a par-3 hole with a lake intervening between the tee and the putting green, A hits three shots into the middle of the lake. He tees up a fourth ball and hits it onto the green, and it rolls into the hole. His score for the hole is _____.

B. B drives out of bounds from the tee. She tees another ball and hits it into the rough 150 yards from the tee. After searching the time limit, she declares the ball lost. She goes back to the tee and is shooting stroke _____.

C. A's third shot is in a bunker adjacent to the putting green. While addressing the ball for his fourth shot, he accidentally touches the sand. He hits the ball onto the green and takes one putt. His score for the hole is _____.

D. B hits her tee shot out of bounds. She tees another ball and tears out some grass back of the ball. She drives into a creek 10 yards in front of the tee. She tees up another ball and drives it onto the fairway. Her score to this point is _____.

E. A's ball lies three on the putting green, 18 inches from the hole. He fails to sink the short putt, leaving the ball on the edge of the hole. In disgust, he hits the ball into the hole with the handle of the putter. His score for the hole is _____.

F. B's ball lies 3 feet off the putting green in two strokes. Without moving the ball, she reaches down and removes a spot of mud from the top of the ball. She chips onto the green and takes one putt. Her score for the hole is _____.

G. A's ball is on the putting green in three shots. He putts the ball, and it comes to rest overhanging the hole. A walks to the hole and waits 15 seconds. The ball then drops into the hole. His score for the hole is _____.

H. A hits his first shot into the sand in a bunker. He hits his next shot, and the ball remains in the bunker. He hits the ball again, and it lands on the green. He discovers that he has hit the wrong ball. He goes back into the bunker and hits the correct ball onto the green and takes two putts. His score for the hole is _____.

I. B hits her drive into the rough. Unsure of whether the ball she finds is hers, she announces her intention to identify the ball. Without marking the ball, she reaches down and rotates the ball without changing its position. After deciding it is the correct ball, she hits it onto the green and takes two putts. Her score for the hole is _____.

J. A's second shot lies in a near-perfect position on the fairway. He takes a practice swing and accidentally touches and moves the ball into a divot hole. He picks up the ball, wipes a spot of mud from it, and replaces it to the original good lie. He chips onto the green and takes one putt. His score for the hole is _____.

Answer Key

1. D
2. NP
3. LH
4. 2SP
5. 2SP on hole 6
6. LH on hole 6
7. NP
8. LH
9. –10.2SP
11. 2SP on hole 3
12. NP
13. LH (B)
14. –16. NP
17. 2SP
18. 2SP (A and B)
19. –20. NP
21. NP (A may require B to replay shot)
22. –23. NP
24. SD (Out of bounds penalty only)
25. 2SP (Tee between markers)
26. 1SP (Count miss, replace ball)
27. NP
28. 2SP
29. LH
30. NP
31. –33. 2SP
34. LH
35. –36. NP
37. LH
38. –39. 2SP
40. LH
41. NP (Replace ball)
42. –43. 2SP
44. –45. NP
46. 2SP

47. LH (A)
48. NP
49. –50. NP (Replace ball)
51. 1SP (Replace ball)
52. 2SP (A) (Replace ball–B)
53. –54. NP (Replace ball—B)
55. 1SP (Replace ball, mark correctly)
56. 1SP
57. 1SP (Replace ball)
58. 2SP
59. NP
60. NP (Replace ball)
61. NP
62. –63. 1SP
64. NP
65. LH
66. –67. NP
68. 2SP
69. 1SP
70. SD (Play from X)
71. SD
72. NP
73. SD (Ball on fairway in play)
74. 1SP
75. SD (Second ball in play)
A. 7
B. 5
C. 7
D. 5
E. 7
F. –G. 5
H. 4
I. 5
J. 6

Index

Par, 2–4, 69
Pitch shot. *See* Approach shot
Pivot, 33, 44, 59
Playing golf, improvement in, 79–93
Playing hints, 89–91
    charting scores, 80
    instructions for the new player, 92
Practice suggestions, 33, 48–49, 58–59, 70–71
Putting, 65–71
    addressing the ball, 65–67
    aiming and judging, 68–69
    importance of, 69
    practice of, 70–71
    swing, 67–68

Relaxation, 33, 55–56, 58, 65, 89–90
Review questions, 9, 13, 21, 37, 50, 64, 71,
        77, 93, 110
Rough, playing from, 76
Rules, 98–108
    general, 100–102
    handicap, 108–9
    hazards, 104–5
    lost ball, 106
    match play, 99
    out of bounds, 106
    provisional ball, 107
    putting green, 103
    rules tests and answers, 121–27
    stroke play, 99
    teeing off, 99–100
    United States Golf Association (USGA),
        98, 108–9
    unplayable ball, 107–8
Safety measures, 11–13, 98

Score card, 4, 99
Slice, correction of, 86–88
Snead, Sam, 60
Speed, clubhead, 55–56
Stance
    checkpoints, 30–32
    effect on ball flight, 42, 88
    steps in taking, 28–30
    types of, 28
Stone, Beth, 63
Swing, the
    full, 51–54
    pattern of, 16–17
    putting, 67–68
    short approach shots, 39–45

Tension
    avoiding, 26, 33
    relation to swing performance, 26, 55–56
Timing, 56
Topping
    cause of, 17, 84
    correction of, 83–84

Waggle, 52
Warming up, 19, 33, 81, 89
Wind, playing in the, 76–77
Woods, 7–8, 109–10
    selection of, for play, 57
Wrist action, 42–44